HAMLET AND OEDIPUS

HAMLET AND OEDIPUS

by

ERNEST JONES, M.D., F.R.C.P.

W · W · NORTON & COMPANY

New York · London

COPYRIGHT © 1949 BY ERNEST JONES

First published in the Norton Library 1976

W. W. Norton & Company, Inc., also publishes *The Norton Anthology of English Literature*, edited by M. H. Abrams et al; *The Norton Anthology of Poetry*, edited by Arthur M. Eastman et al; *World Masterpieces*, edited by Maynard Mack et al; *The Norton Reader*, edited by Arthur M. Eastman et al; *The Norton Facsimile of the First Folio of Shakespeare*, prepared by Charlton Hinman; *The Norton Anthology of Modern Poetry*, edited by Richard Ellmann and Robert O'Clair; *The Norton Anthology of Short Fiction*, edited by R. V. Cassill; *The Norton Anthology of American Literature*, edited by Ronald Gottesman et al; and the *Norton Critical Editions*.

W. W. Norton & Company, Inc., 500 Fifth Avenue, New York, N.Y. 10110

Library of Congress Cataloging in Publication Data

Jones, Ernest, 1879-1958.
    Hamlet and Oedipus.

    (The Norton library)
    Includes bibliographical references and index.
    1. Shakespeare, William, 1564-1616. Hamlet.
2. Psychoanalysis in literature. I. Title.
PR2807.J63 1976   822.3'3   75-42371
ISBN 0-393-00799-5

Printed in the United States of America
3 4 5 6 7 8 9 0

TO

MY WIFE KATHERINE

MY

CONSTANT HELPMEET

CONTENTS

PREFACE

THIS ESSAY, first written forty years ago as an exposition of a footnote in Freud's "Traumdeutung" (1900), has had a somewhat curious career. It was first published under the title " The Oedipus Complex as an Explanation of Hamlet's Mystery" in *The American Journal of Psychology*, January 1910. A German translation of this appeared in the following year as a brochure in the series *Schriften zur angewandten Seelenkunde* under the title "Das Problem des Hamlet und der Oedipus-Komplex". In 1923, under the title "A Psycho-Analytic Study of Hamlet", it formed the first chapter of my Essays in Applied Psycho-Analysis, now long out of print. On each occasion, as with the present version, I have revised and extended it. I am obliged to the previous publishers for permission to make use of the material again.

It will be admitted that none of these publications was particularly accessible to the general literary public, so that I feel justified in presenting once more, and this time in both a more complete and a more available form, the psycho-analytical theory of Hamlet; the general revival of interest in the Hamlet play has also emboldened me. Somehow or other the news that such an interpretation of Hamlet's difficulty exists has spread fairly widely, and I have frequently had to express my regret to would-be students of it that their wish to read the original account has been so hard to gratify.

In quotations from "Hamlet" I have used Shakespeare's punctuation as restored by Professor Dover Wilson.

That sexual needs and passions may at times be related

to murderous impulses has of course long been known. Only since Freud's work, however, have we learned that corresponding elements commonly operate in the infant's mind before the damping down that evolution into childhood brings; and, further, that the conflicts then aroused, though remaining repressed in the unconscious, may profoundly affect adult life. This theme I had to introduce into my essay somewhat circumspectly forty years ago, when such knowledge was confined to a minute group, and even so it met with much hard abuse. To-day in a more enlightened age I may count on its impact being far less startling.

CHAPTER I

PSYCHOLOGY AND AESTHETICS

Psychologists have as yet devoted relatively little attention to individual analytic study of genius and of artistic creativeness, and have mainly confined themselves to observations of a general order. They seem to share the shyness or even aversion displayed by the world at large against too searching an analysis of a thing of beauty, the feeling expressed in Keats' lines on the prismatic study of the rainbow. The fear that beauty may vanish under too scrutinizing a gaze, and with it our pleasure, is, however, only in part justified; much depends on the nature of the pleasure and on the attitude of the analyst. Experience has shown that intellectual appreciation in particular is only heightened by understanding, and to further this is one of the recognized social functions of the critic. Since, moreover, intellectual appreciation comprises an important part of the higher forms of aesthetic appreciation, a deepened understanding can but increase this also.

It has been found that with poetic creations this critical procedure cannot halt at the work of art itself: to isolate this from its creator is to impose artificial limits to our understanding of it. It has, it is true, been rather fashionable of late to assert that every work should be judged "purely on its merits" independently of any knowledge of its author. Presumably this came of a protest, healthy enough in itself, against the artistic snobbery that would judge works of art solely by the fame of their authors. Nevertheless, all serious critics know that the appreciation of a work and an understanding of its intention are only heightened when it is related to some knowledge of its author's characteristics and to the stages in his artistic development. As Masson,[1] in defending his biographical analysis of Shakespeare, justly says: "not till every poem has been, as it were, chased up to the moment of its organic origin, and resolved into the mood or intention, or constitutional reverie, out of which it sprang, will its import be adequately felt or understood". A work of art is too often regarded as a finished thing-in-itself, something almost independent of the creator's personality, as if little would be learned about the one or the other by connecting the two studies. Informed criticism, however, shows that a correlated study of the two sheds light in both directions, on the inner nature of the composition and on the creative impulse of its author. The two can be separated only at the expense of diminished appreciation, whereas to increase our knowledge of either automatically deepens our understanding of the other. Masson[2] well says: "What a man shall or can imagine, equally with what he shall or can desire, depends ultimately on his own nature, and so even on his acquisitions and experiences. . . . Imagination is not, after all, creation out of nothing, but only re-combination, at the bidding of moods and of conscious purposes, out of the materials furnished by memory, reading and experience; which materials vary with the individual cases." In asserting this deterministic point of view, one characteristic also of modern clinical psychology, Masson gives us a hint of one of the sources of the prevailing

[1] Masson: Shakespeare Personally, 1914, p. 13.
[2] idem: op. cit., pp. 129, 130.

aversion from psychological analysis—namely, the pre-ference for the belief that poetic ideas arise in their finished form, perhaps from some quasi-divine source, rather than as elaborations of simple and familiar elements devoid in themselves of glamour or aesthetic beauty. This point of view becomes still more com-prehensible when one realizes that the deeper, un-conscious mind, which is doubtless the ultimate source of such ideas, as of all abstract ideas, is comprised of mental material which in its native form is incompatible with the standards of the conscious mind—this being the reason for its being kept "unconscious"—material which has to be extensively transformed and purified before it can be presented to consciousness. In short, it is one more illustration of the constant resistance that man displays against any danger he may be in of apprehending his inner nature.

The artist himself has always avoided a closely analytic attitude towards his work, doubtless for the same reason as the common man. He usually dissociates the impelling motive force from his conscious will, and sometimes even ascribes it to an actual external agency, divine or de-monic. D'Annunzio, for example, in his Flame of Life makes his artist-hero think of "the extraordinary moments in which his hand had written an immortal verse that had seemed to him not born of his brain, but dictated by an impetuous deity to which his un-conscious organ had obeyed like a blind instrument". Nowhere is the irresistible impetuosity of artistic creation more perfectly portrayed than in the memorable passage in Ecce Homo where Nietzsche describes the birth of "Also sprach Zarathustra", and its involuntary character has been plainly indicated by most great philosophers and writers, from Socrates to Goethe. I wish to lay special stress on this feature, on the artist's unawareness of the ultimate source of his creation, since it is cognate to the argument of the present essay.

Within the past few years the analytic investigation of the workings of genius has been infused with fresh interest by the luminous studies of Freud, who has revealed some of the fundamental mechanisms by which artistic and poetic creativeness proceeds.[1] He has shown that the main characteristics of these mechanisms have much in common with those underlying many apparently dissimilar mental processes, such as dreams, wit, and psycho-neurotic symptoms;[2] further, that all these processes bear an intimate relation to fantasy, to the realization of non-conscious wishes, to psychological "repression", to the revival of childhood memories, and to the psycho-sexual life of the individual. It was to be expected that the knowledge so laboriously gained by the psycho-analytic method devised by Freud would prove of great value in the attempt to solve the psychological problems concerned with the obscurer motives of human action and desire. In fact it is hard to think of any other scientific mode of approach to such problems than through the patient dissecting of the deeper and more hidden elements of the mind which is the aim of this procedure. The results already obtained by Abraham,[3]

[1] Freud: Der Wahn und die Träume in W. Jensen's Gradiva, 1907; "Der Dichter und das Phantasieren", *Neue Revue*, 1908, Nr. 10, S. 716; Eine Kindheitserinnerung des Leonardo da Vinci, 1910; "Das Motiv der Kästchenwahl", *Imago*, 1913, S. 257, etc.

[2] idem: Die Traumdeutung, 1900; Der Witz und seine Beziehung zum Unbewussten, 1905; Drei Abhandlungen zur Sexualtheorie, 1905; Sammlung kleiner Schriften, 1906–18.

[3] Abraham: Traum und Mythus. Eine Studie zur Völkerpsychologie, 1909; "Amenhotep IV. Psychoanalytische Beiträge zum Verständnis seiner Persönlichkeit und des monotheistischen Aton-Kultes", *Imago*, 1912, S. 334.

Ferenczi,[1] Hitschmann,[2] Rank,[3] Sadger,[4] and others are only a foretoken of the applications that will be possible when this method has been employed over a larger field than has hitherto been the case.

There are two particular reasons why Freud was in a position to make the contribution he did to what has since been called "depth psychology". One was his invention of a special technique for penetrating to the more obscure regions of the mind. The other was that his professional work was concerned with mental suffering. Experience has shown that no motive exists besides the need to be relieved of suffering that will bring a human being to reveal the truly intimate core of his personality, so that depth psychology has perforce to be medical psychology; other psychologists are, in the nature of things, debarred from exploring those depths from which the more visible parts of the personality have developed and of which they largely remain but radiations. This consideration gives rise to the obvious objection that any conclusions reached by such investigations have their general validity vitiated by their origin in a study of the "abnormal". This quite logical objection, however, lost its force when it was discovered that the neurotic symptoms that had given rise to the suffering proceed from primordial difficulties and conflicts inherent in every mind, and that they are merely one of the many various ways in which attempts are made to cope

[1] Ferenczi: Contributions to Psycho-Analysis (Engl. transl.), 1916.
[2] Hitschmann: Gottfried Keller, 1919.
[3] Rank: Der Künstler. Ansätze zu einer Sexual-Psychologie, 1907; Der Mythus von der Geburt des Helden, 1909; Die Lohengrinsage, 1911; Das Inzest-Motiv in Dichtung und Sage, 1912; Psychoanalytische Beiträge zur Mythenforschung, 1919.
[4] Sadger: Konrad Ferdinand Meyer. Eine pathographisch-psychologische Studie, 1908; Aus dem Leibesleben Nicolaus Lenaus, 1909; Friedrich Hebbel, 1920.

with these; the character traits and peculiarities of the so-called "normal" person, for instance, which are commonly defensive in nature, proceed from exactly the same source as do neurotic symptoms.

In the present excursus, moreover, such an objection is even less relevant than elsewhere, since the problem to be discussed, namely, the meaning of Hamlet's conflicts and suffering, has been widely recognized by literary critics to be a psycho-pathological one; the play is mainly concerned with a hero's unavailing fight against what can only be called a disordered mind. Hence it is surely appropriate for a medical psychologist to offer a contribution based on his special knowledge of the deeper layers of the mind where such disorders arise. Many attempts, as we shall see, have been made by psychiatrists to deal with the problem along medical lines, but, since they have usually considered it in terms merely of clinical diagnosis, their efforts have in no way illuminated our understanding of what is really going on in Hamlet's mind.

Before we approach our task there is one further consideration to be taken into account. Although a few psycho-analytic studies have been undertaken in other fields of art, such as Freud's,[1] of Michael Angelo's statue of Moses, or my own on the painters Andrea del Sarto[2] and Simone Martini,[3] it is in the nature of things that most of such studies have been concerned with poets, whose productions, cast in ideational form, are

[1] Freud: "Der Moses des Michelangelo", *Imago*, Jahrg. III, 1914, S. 15.

[2] Ernest Jones: "The Influence of Andrea del Sarto's Wife on his Art", *Imago*, 1913. Reprinted as Chapter VI in Essays in Applied Psycho-Analysis, 1923.

[3] idem: "The Madonna's Conception through the Ear", *Jahrbuch für Psychoanalyse*, 1914. Reprinted as Chapter VIII in Essays in Applied Psycho-Analysis, 1923.

more accessible to intellectual understanding. In the case of dramatic art, however, with which we shall have more to do, there is a special feature. Characters are created whose impersonating representatives act and move on the stage, and we are asked to believe that they are living persons; indeed, the dramatist's success is largely measured by this criterion, one in which Shakespeare was superbly pre-eminent. Now to what extent may one discuss such a character in the psychological terms applicable to a living person, and in what sense would this procedure ever be valid? True enough, the audience feels itself very free in this respect, and on leaving the theatre one may frequently hear such comments as "I believe the real reason why he did it must have been because he thought so-and-so, although that doesn't actually come out in the play". Literary and dramatic critics also have freely adopted this convention, and much of the discussion of the consistency of a given character turns on the assumption that he was alive. And all this notwithstanding our knowledge that he has never existed save in the dramatist's imagination.

On the other hand, vigorous protests have been made against this very procedure, and we are bidden remember that the character has no objective existence. A. B. Walkley,[1] for instance, the distinguished dramatic critic, inveighs caustically against Bradley's assumption that Hamlet had lived before the play opens, and counts it as one of the illusions of the Romantic Age. Actually Goethe was one of the first to speculate on what sort of young man Hamlet had been before his misfortunes crowded upon him, and his delineation of this period in his supposed life has never been surpassed. Professor

[1] A. B. Walkley: Drama and Life, 1908.

Dover Wilson,[1] for whose work one can feel nothing but profound respect and gratitude, has in his turn accused me of the same fallacy, although he somewhat inconsistently goes on to fall a victim to it himself by interpreting—and very skilfully—what he supposes went on in Hamlet's mind at various stages of the action. The charge, however, would seem to go very wide of the mark. No dramatic criticism of the personae in a play is possible except under the pretence that they are living people, and surely one is well aware of this pretence. Again, if a psychologist is asked to comment on a certain man's behaviour in a particular emergency or his response to various situations, especially if these are described in great detail, he would often be able to say something about what that man's character and temperament must have been *before* the events in question. A psycho-analyst can often go further and say something about the man's early development, since early experiences leave a deeper imprint than later ones; they are also far more limited in kind than the later ones and are very familiar to those who have studied them. If a man reacts powerfully to a given situation, then the way in which he does so must be influenced by previous experiences of a kind that somehow correspond with it by an associative likeness; fresh experiences, however novel, are always assimilated by the unconscious mind to older ones. In other words, the current response is always compounded partly of a response to the actual situation and partly of past responses to older situations that are unconsciously felt to be similar.

My answer is, therefore, that in so far and in the same sense as a character in a play is taken as being a living

[1] J. Dover Wilson: Hamlet, 2nd Edition, 1936, Introduction, p. xlv.

person, to that extent must he have had a life before
the action in the play began, since no one starts life as an
adult. Often, of course, we are informed of an earlier
life. We could not face the depth of King Lear's forlorn-
ness and despair did we not know something of the
former majesty of his reign and his kindness to his
daughters, and even of Hamlet we are told of his studies
in Wittenberg. But an artist does not convey all he wishes
to solely in matter-of-fact literalness; if he left nothing to
our imagination he would fail to stir it. Our response to
his creative effort always implies a reading between the
lines on our part, an extension of what he has actually
written—provided always that our imagination is in tune
with his and never departs from it. A final proviso!
An artist has an unconscious mind as well as a conscious
one, and his imagination springs at least as fully from
the former as from the latter.

For these reasons I propose to pretend that Hamlet was
a living person—one might parenthetically add that to
most of us he is more so than many a player on the stage
of life—and inquire what measure of man such a person
must have been to feel and act in certain situations in the
way Shakespeare tells us he did. So far shall I be from
forgetting that he was a figment of Shakespeare's mind
that I shall then go on to consider the relation of this
particular imaginative creation to the personality of
Shakespeare himself.

CHAPTER II

THE PROBLEM OF HAMLET AND THE EXPLANATIONS PROFFERED

THE PARTICULAR problem of Hamlet, with which this essay is concerned, is intimately related to some of the most frequently recurring problems that are presented in the course of psycho-analytic work, and it has thus seemed possible to secure a fresh point of view from which an answer might be proffered to questions that have baffled attempts made along less technical lines. Some of the most competent literary authorities have freely acknowledged the inadequacy of all the solutions of the problem that have hitherto been suggested, and when judged by psychological standards their in-adequacy is still more evident. The aim of the present essay is to expound and bring into relation with other work an hypothesis suggested many years ago by Freud in a footnote to his Traumdeutung.[1] Before attempting this it will be necessary to make a few general remarks about the nature of the problem and the previous solutions that have been offered.

The problem presented by the tragedy of "Hamlet" is one of peculiar interest in at least two respects. In the first place, the play is almost universally considered to be the chief masterpiece of one of the greatest minds the world has known. It probably expresses the core of Shakespeare's philosophy and outlook on life as no other work of his does. Bradley[2] writes, for instance: "Hamlet

---

[1] Freud: Die Traumdeutung, 1900, S. 183.
[2] Bradley: Oxford Lectures on Poetry, 1909, p. 357.

is the most fascinating character, and the most in-exhaustible, in all imaginative literature. What else should he be, if the world's greatest poet, who was able to give almost the reality of nature to creations totally unlike himself, put his own soul straight into this creation, and when he wrote Hamlet's speeches wrote down his own heart?" Figgis[1] calls Hamlet "Shakespeare's completest declaration of himself". Taine's[2] opinion also was that "Hamlet is Shakespeare, and at the close of a gallery of portraits, which have all some features of his own, Shakespeare has painted himself in the most striking of them all". It may be expected, therefore, that anything which will give us the key to the inner meaning of the tragedy will necessarily provide a clue to much of the deeper workings of Shakespeare's mind.

In the second place, the intrinsic interest of the play itself is exceedingly great. Already in 1711 the then Lord Shaftesbury could describe it[3] as "that piece which appears to have most affected English hearts and has perhaps been oftenest acted of any which have come upon our stage". Since then, of course, its fame has become world-wide, and it has moved countless millions. This universal appeal shows that its inmost theme must contain something to which the heart of mankind in general reverberates, and there is little doubt that this resides in the personality of the hero. Bradby[4] truly calls him "a central figure of surpassing interest and genius, which has gripped the imagination of the learned and the unlearned in all ages and which will continue to fascinate

[1] Darrell Figgis: Shakespeare: A Study, 1911, p. 320.
[2] Taine: Histoire de la Littérature Anglaise, 1866, t. 11, p. 254. See also K. Götz: Das Hamlet-Mysterium, 1903, and many other writers.
[3] Quoted by Stoll: Shakespeare and other Masters, 1940.
[4] C. F. Bradby: The Problems of Hamlet, 1928, p. 60.

so long as the mind of man is haunted by the mystery of life and death". Dover Wilson[1] gives as his opinion that the understanding of Shakespeare's "Hamlet" is the greatest of all literary problems. Of the hero he says[2] that "to spectators in the theatre he is more convincingly life-like than any other character in literature".

The interest of the play and its hero is far from being confined to the field of drama. More has been written about Hamlet than about any other character of fiction; more, it has been said, than about anyone who actually lived with the exception of Jesus Christ, Napoleon, and of course Shakespeare himself. Those who have had to wade through this spate of literature, however, will probably agree that much of it is of singularly poor quality and that the real serious contributors can almost be counted on the fingers of two hands; indeed, if we contented ourselves with the names of Brandes, Dowden, Furnivall, Loening, Bradley, and Dover Wilson one hand would almost suffice. The central mystery in it—namely, the meaning of Hamlet's hesitancy in seeking to obtain revenge for his father's murder—has well been called the Sphinx of modern Literature.[3] It has given rise to a regiment of hypotheses and to a large library of critical and controversial literature. No detailed account of them will here be attempted, since it is obtainable in the writings of Loening,[4] Döring,[5] and others,[6] but the main

[1] Dover Wilson: op. cit., p. xi.
[2] Idem: What Happens in "Hamlet", 1925, p. 219.
[3] It is but fitting that Freud should have solved the riddle of this Sphinx, as he has that of the Theban one.
[4] Loening: Die Hamlet-Tragödie Shakespeares, 1893. This book is especially to be recommended, for it is certainly the most critical work on the subject. [Since the painstaking and rewarding labours of Prof. Dover Wilson this sentence is no longer valid.]
[5] Döring: 'Ein Jahrhundert deutscher Hamlet-Kritik', Die Kritik, 1897, Nr. 131.
[6] If it is ever completed, Schick's "Das Corpus Hamleticum" will

points of view that have been put forward must be briefly mentioned.

To begin with, are we sure that there is any delay, or does Hamlet perform his task as swiftly as can reasonably be expected? The desperate attempt has been made, e.g. by J. M. Robertson,[1] to deny the existence of any delay, only, however, for it to be found necessary on the very next page to admit it and propound a reason for it. Then there is what might flippantly be called the box-office view that the culminating point of a tragedy, especially when this takes the form of a murder, usually comes at the end, so that to make a play long enough to satisfy the audience it has to be dragged out to a present-able length.[2] Even so acute a writer as Santayana[3] attributes the delay to the necessity to prolong the play. Again, there is the view that any apparent delay is not inherent in Shakespeare's intention, but occurs because of his superimposing his own work, i.e. spiritual exposition of the characters, on a primitive revenge theme which he did not eliminate, but in which he was presumably not very interested. According to Stoll,[4] for instance, "The dramatist could not (if he would) change the popular old story; the capital deed must, as there and in all other revenge plays, ancient or modern, come at the end. Therefore Shakespeare motives this postponement of the catastrophe by the hero's self-reproaches, not in the sense of grounding it in character, but of explaining it and bridging it over; by these reminders he makes the audience feel that the

---

be the most comprehensive. So far the first five volumes deal only with the mythology of the old legend!

[1] J. M. Robertson: The Problem of "Hamlet", 1919, pp. 16, 17.
[2] See, for instance, *The New Age*, Feb. 22, 1912.
[3] Santayana: "Hamlet" in his Life and Letters, Vol. I, 1928.
[4] E. E. Stoll: Hamlet the Man, 1919, p. 3.

main business in hand is, though retarded, not lost to view".

Of the solutions that have been offered many will probably be remembered on account of their very extravagance.[1] Allied if not belonging to this group are the hypotheses that see in Hamlet only allegorical tendencies of various kinds. Thus Gerth[2] sees in the play an elaborate defence of Protestantism; Gerkrath,[3] an expression of the revolt emanating in Wittenberg against Roman Catholicism and feudalism; Rio,[4] Spanier,[5] and Tucker,[6] on the contrary, a defence of Roman Catholicism. Meisels,[7] however, claims Hamlet as a typical Jew. According to him the play is "a focus on which is concentrated all the thought and feeling, the plaints and sighs, of a people bleeding from the heart at the injuries inflicted by the wickedness of the world". John Owen[8] treats the play as an exposition of Montaigne's scepticism and regards the consummation of the

---

[1] Such as, for instance, the view developed by Vining (The Mystery of Hamlet, 1881) that Hamlet's weakness is to be explained by the fact that he was a woman wrongly brought up as a man. An American doctor, misreading the phrase "fat and scant of breath", wrote an article explaining that Hamlet's hesitancy was due to "a redundance of adipose matter which weakens and impedes the power of the will". He found indications that Hamlet was suffering from fatty degeration of the heart. (E. V. Blake: "The Impediment of Adipose; a Celebrated Case", Popular Science Monthly, 1880, p. 60.)

[2] Gerth: Der Hamlet von Shakespeare, 1861.

[3] Elisabeth Gerkrath: Das dramatische Meisterwerk des Protestantismus, 1918.

[4] Rio: Shakespeare, 1864.

[5] Spanier: Der "Papist" Shakespeare im Hamlet, 1890.

[6] W. J. Tucker: The Masterpiece "Hamlet", in College Shakespeare, 1932.

[7] S. Meisels: "Judenhamlet", Populär-wissenschaftliche Monatsblätter zur Belehrung über das Judentum, 1901.

[8] John Owen: The Five Great Skeptical Dramas of History, 1896.

tragedy as purely accidental. Stedefeld,[1] however, regards it as a protest against the scepticism of Montaigne, Feis[2] as one against his mysticism and bigotry. A writer under the name of Mercade[3] maintains that the play is an allegorical philosophy of history: Hamlet is the spirit of truth-seeking which realizes itself historically as progress, Claudius is the type of evil and error, Ophelia is the Church, Polonius its Absolutism and Tradition, the Ghost is the ideal voice of Christianity, Fortinbras is Liberty, and so on. Many writers, including Plumptre[4] and Silberschlag,[5] have read the play as a satire on Mary, Queen of Scots, and her marriage with Bothwell after the murder of Darnley, and Winstanley[6] has recently made out a case for the view that the figure of Hamlet was largely taken from that of James VI of Scotland, the heir to the English throne; while Elze,[7] Isaac,[8] and others have found in it a relation to the Earl of Essex's domestic experiences, and McNabb[9] a defence of him. Such explications overlook a characteristic of all Shakespeare's works, and indeed those of any great

[1] Stedefeld: Hamlet, ein Tendenzdrama Shakespeare's gegen die skeptische und kosmopolitische Weltanschauung des M. de Montaigne, 1871.

[2] Feis: Shakspere and Montaigne, 1884. The importance of Montaigne's influence on Shakespeare, as shown in Hamlet, was first remarked by Sterling (*London and Westminster Review*, 1838, p. 321), and has been clearly pointed out by J. M. Robertson, in his book "Montaigne and Shakespeare", 1897. See also S. Türck: Shakespeare und Montaigne. Ein Beitrag zur Hamlet-Frage, 1930.

[3] Mercade: Hamlet; or Shakespeare's Philosophy of History, 1875.   [4] Plumptre: Observations on Hamlet, 1796.

[5] K. Silberschlag: "Shakespeare's Hamlet", *Morgenblatt*, 1860, Nr. 46, 47, and "Shakespeare's Hamlet, seine Quellen und politischen Beziehungen", *Shakespeare Jahrbuch*, 1877, S. 261.

[6] Lilian Winstanley: Hamlet and the Scottish Succession, 1921.

[7] Elze: *Shakespeare Jahrbuch*, Bd. III.

[8] Isaac: *Shakespeare Jahrbuch*, Bd. XVI.

[9] V. McNabb: "Is Hamlet Autobiography?", *Catholic World*, 1915, p. 754.

artist—namely, the subordination of either current or
tendentious interests to the inspiration of the work as an
artistic whole.

The most important hypotheses that have been put
forward are sub-varieties of three main points of view.
The first of these sees the difficulty about the performance
of the task in Hamlet's character, which is not fitted
for effective action of any kind; the second sees it in the
nature of the task, which is such as to be almost impossible
of performance by any one; and the third in some
special feature of the task that renders it peculiarly
difficult or repugnant to someone of Hamlet's particular
temperament.

The *first* of these views, sometimes called the "subjective" one, which would trace the inhibition to some
general defect in Hamlet's constitution, was independently elaborated more than a century ago by Mackenzie,[1] Goethe,[2] Coleridge,[3] and Schlegel.[4] Partly because
of its association with Goethe, who promulgated the
view as a young man when under the influence of
Herder[5] (who, by the way, later abandoned it[6]), it has
been the most widely held view of Hamlet, and he has
most often been represented on the stage in this light.
Hardly any literary authorities, however, have held it in
its pure form in the past half century, though in 1850
Gervinus[7] could still write: "Since this riddle has been
solved by Goethe in his Wilhelm Meister, we can scarcely

---

[1] Henry Mackenzie: *The Mirror*, April 18, 1780.
[2] Goethe: Wilhelm Meister's Lehrjahre, 1795, Bd. IV, Kap. XIII.
[3] Coleridge: Lectures on Shakespeare, 1808.
[4] Schlegel: Vorlesungen über dramatische Kunst und Litteratur,
III, 1809.   [5] Herder: Von deutscher Art und Kunst, 1773.
[6] Idem: Aufsatz über Shakespeare im dritten Stück der Adrastea,
1801.
[7] Gervinus: Shakespeare, Dritte Auflage, Bd. II, S. 98, Engl.
transl., p. 550.

conceive that it was one". Türck[1] suggestively remarks that Goethe's view of Hamlet was a projected account of his own Werther. The oft-quoted passage describing Hamlet runs as follows: "To me it is clear that Shakespeare meant to present a great deed imposed as a duty upon a soul that is not equal to it. Here is an oak-tree planted in a costly vase that should have nurtured only the most delicate flowers: the roots expand; the vase is shattered. A too pure, noble, highly moral nature, but without that energy of nerve which constitutes the hero, sinks under a burden which it can neither bear nor renounce".[2]

Thus the view essentially is that Hamlet, for temperamental reasons, was inherently incapable of decisive action of any kind. These temperamental reasons are variously stated by different writers: by Mackenzie as "an extreme sensibility of mind apt to be too strongly impressed by its situation, and overpowered by the feelings which that situation excites", by Goethe as "over-sensitiveness", by Coleridge as "overbalance in the contemplative faculty", by Schlegel as "reflective deliberation—often a pretext to cover cowardice and lack of decision", by Vischer[3] as "melancholic disposition", and so on; Trench[4] describes Hamlet as "a man of contemplation reacting only mentally, being from the first incapable of the required action". Boas[5] calls him "a man of genius, with a will atrophied through an abnormal development, not only of the reflective, but

---

[1] Herman Türck: Das psychologische Problem in der Hamlet-Tragödie, 1890, S. 8.
[2] Goethe: Wilhelm Meisters Lehrjahre. Viertes Buch, Kap. 13.
[3] Vischer: Kritische Gänge. Neue Folge. 1861, Heft. 2.
[4] W. F. Trench: Shakespeare's Hamlet: A New Commentary, 1913, pp. 74–9, 119, 137.
[5] F. S. Boas: "Hamlet" in Shakespeare and his Predecessors, 1896, p. 407.

of the emotional faculties", Semler[1] on the other hand considering that he lacks passion (!), and Stewart[2] also that he is incapacitated from enduring emotion. Sir Edmund Chambers[3] speaks of the play as "the tragedy of the *intellectuel*, of the impotence of the over-cultivated imagination and the over-subtilized reasoning powers to meet the call of everyday life for practical efficiency". Many authors, e.g. Konrad Meier,[4] make the philosophy and humanism of Wittenberg responsible for this one-sided intellectual development, and Barnay[5] considers the conflict between the impulse to act and to reflect was due to his being a Dane by birth but then being influenced by the German teaching at Wittenberg.

There is probably more truth in the conception of Hamlet as a man whose powers of imagination were so intense as often to take the place of action. Kuno Fischer[6] attributes to him an abundance of feeling, which can rise to excitement: "When a passion can expend itself in words it is less apt to result in deeds". Otto Rank,[7] who labels Hamlet as a "Phantasiemensch", explains many critical passages in the play in terms of Hamlet's acting in his imagination being to him equivalent to acting in reality. One might here recall the not unimportant fact that Shakespeare himself was by profession

---

[1] Christian Semler: Shakespeare's Hamlet. Die Weltanschauung und der Styl des Dichters, 1879.

[2] C. D. Stewart: "The Mystery of Hamlet" in Some Textual Difficulties in Shakespeare, 1914.

[3] E. K. Chambers: "Hamlet" in Shakespeare: A Survey, 1925, p. 182.

[4] Konrad Meier: "Klassisches in Hamlet", *Vierter Jahresbericht des König Georgs Gymnasiums*, 1907.

[5] L. Barnay: "Zur Darstellung des Hamlet", *Deutsche Revue*, 1901, S. 103.

[6] Kuno Fischer: "Shakespeare's Hamlet", Kleine Schriften, V. 1896, S. 206.

[7] Otto Rank: "Das Schauspiel in 'Hamlet' ", *Imago*, Bd. IV, S. 41.

an actor, i.e. someone who can live experiences vicariously and with whom words are often the equivalent of deeds. The terms "introspection" and "introversion", so popular nowadays, also come to one's mind. A very pejorative, and definitely biased, interpretation of them has recently appeared in a book by Madariaga,[1] where it is maintained that Hamlet was a monster of selfishness and cruelty, who never did anything from a sense of duty but only when his immediate personal interests were concerned. This makes the play, according to Madariaga, "all clear as crystal". We approach here the psychopathological aspect of Hamlet, about which something will be said later. This again may be divided into the "constitutional" view, Hamlet being by nature unstable, and the "shock" view, where Hamlet, a previously happy normal man, is so paralysed by the news of his father's death and murder as to be incapable of any action. This latter view is expressed by Adams[2]: Hamlet possesses to a fatal extent idealism regarding human nature, and this is subjected to a terrible disillusionment. The effect is in both cases the same, a general inhibition of will power. Clutton-Brock,[3] evidently influenced by the recent teaching of "shell shock", also talks of the nervous shock from the Ghost's news, and more specifically considers that this is a "repression" so that Hamlet flinches whenever reminded of the painful topic and avoids it to the best of his ability.

Guha[4] maintains that Hamlet, being convinced that he cannot reform the whole rotten world, thinks that

---

[1] S. de Madariaga: On Hamlet, 1948.
[2] J. Q. Adams: Commentary in his edition of "Hamlet", 1929, p. 193.
[3] A. Clutton-Brock: Shakespeare's "Hamlet," 1922, p. 45.
[4] P. K. Guha: On Two Problems in Shakespeare, 1926.

vengeance on the King is merely futile; Türck[1] holds a similar view. Wolff[2] similarly ascribes Hamlet's attitude to scorn of the world and consequent unwillingness to take part in its affairs; so he takes refuge in theatrical acting instead. According to Venable,[3] Hamlet's idealism is concerned with the eternal and is above mere personal revenge.

It will be noticed that while some of these writers lay stress on the over-sensitiveness of feeling, others think rather of an unduly developed mental activity. A view fairly representative of the pure Coleridge school,[4] for instance, would run somewhat as follows: Owing to his highly developed intellectual powers, Hamlet could never take a simple or single view of any question, but always saw a number of different aspects and possible explanations with every problem. A given course of action never seemed to him unequivocal and obvious, so that in practical life his scepticism and reflective powers paralysed his conduct. He thus stands for what may roughly be called the type of an intellect over-developed at the expense of the will, and in the Germany of the past he was frequently held up as a warning example to university professors who showed signs of losing themselves in abstract trains of thought at the risk of diminished contact with external reality.[5]

---

[1] H. Türck: "Das psychologische Problem in der Hamlet-Tragödie", Faust-Hamlet-Christus, 1918, S. 201.

[2] G. Wolff: Der Fall Hamlet, 1914.

[3] E. Venable: The Hamlet Problem and its Solution, 1912.

[4] An expanded account of Coleridge's view is given by Edward Strachey: Shakespeare's Hamlet: An Attempt to find the Key to a Great Moral Problem by Methodical Analysis of the Play, 1848.

[5] See for instance Köstlin: "Shakespeare und Hamlet", Morgenblatt, 1864, Nr. 25, 26. Already in 1816 Börne in his Dramaturgische Blättern had amusingly developed this idea. He closes one article with the words " If it had been a German who had written Hamlet I should not have been at all surprised. A German would

There are at least three grave objections to this view of Hamlet's hesitancy; one based on general psychological considerations and the others on objective evidence furnished by the text of the play. It is true that at first sight increasing scepticism and reflection might appear to weaken motive, inasmuch as they tear aside common illusions concerning the value of certain lines of conduct; this is seen, for example, in such a matter as social reform, where a man's energy in carrying out minor philanthropic undertakings may wane in proportion to the amount of clear thought he gives to the problems. But closer consideration will show that this debilitation is a qualitative rather than a quantitative one. Scepticism merely leads to a simplification of motive in general, and to a reduction in the number of those motives that are efficacious; it brings about a lack of adherence to certain conventional ones rather than a general failure in the springs of action. Every student of individual psychology knows that any such general weakening in energy is invariably due to other causes than intellectual scepticism—namely, to the results of buried intra-psychical conflicts. This train of thought need not be further developed here, for it is really irrelevant to discuss the cause of Hamlet's general aboulia if, as will presently be maintained, this did not exist; the argument, then, must remain unconvincing except to those who already apprehend its validity.

Unequivocal evidence of the inadequacy of the hypothesis under discussion, however, may be obtained from perusal of the play. In the first place, as was first em-

---

need only a fine legible hand for it. He describes himself and there you have Hamlet." Frank Harris (The Man Shakespeare and his Tragic Life-Story, 1909, p. 267) writes that Hamlet "became a type for ever of the philosopher or man of letters who, by thinking, has lost the capacity for action."

phatically pointed out by Hartley Coleridge,[1] there is every reason to believe that, apart from the task in question, Hamlet is a man capable of very decisive action, with no compunction whatever about killing. This could be not only impulsive, as in the killing of Polonius, but deliberate, as in the arranging for the death of Guildenstern and Rosencrantz. His biting scorn and mockery towards his enemies, and even towards Ophelia, his cutting denunciation of his mother, his lack of remorse after the death of Polonius; these are not signs of a gentle, yielding, or weak nature. His mind was as rapidly made up about the organization of the drama to be acted before his uncle, as it was resolutely made up when the unpleasant task had to be performed of breaking with the no longer congenial Ophelia. He shows no trace of hesitation when he stabs the listener behind the curtain,[2] when he makes his violent onslaught on the pirates, leaps into the grave with Laertes or accepts his challenge to what he must know was a duel, or when he follows his father's spirit on to the battlements;[3] nor is there any

---

[1] Hartley Coleridge: "On the Character of Hamlet", *Blackwood's Magazine*, 1828.

[2] I find Loening's detailed argument quite conclusive that Hamlet did not have the king in his mind when he struck this blow (op. cit., S. 242-4, 362-3). After all, he had just left the king engrossed in prayer, and the latter could hardly have rushed in front of him to the bedroom. The words that have given rise to the common misunderstanding ("I know not. Is it the king?") are surely to be read as a response to his mother's alarm, combined with a typically irrational "wish-fulfilment" that his task has by a lucky accident been accomplished. "Thou wretched, rash, intruding fool, farewell: (insert: for a moment) I took thee for the better" comes then when he realizes the impossibility of his previous thought (or wish). Soon after this the ghost appears, which would have been superfluous had Hamlet seriously intended to kill the king, and Hamlet admits his recalcitrance.

[3] Meadows (Hamlet, 1871) considers that Hamlet's behaviour on this occasion is the strongest proof of his mental health and vigour.

lack of determination in his resolution to meet the ghost:

> I'll speak to it though hell itself should gape
> And bid me hold my peace;

or in his cry when Horatio clings to him:

> Unhand me gentlemen,
> By heaven I'll make a ghost of him that lets me!
> I say, away!

On none of these occasions do we find any sign of that paralysis of doubt which has so frequently been imputed to him. On the contrary, not once is there any sort of failure in moral or physical courage except only in the matter of the revenge. Bradley, who calls Hamlet "a heroic, terrible figure",[1] writes of the Coleridge view:[2] "The theory describes, therefore, a man in certain respects like Coleridge himself, on one side a man of genius, on the other side, the side of will, deplorably weak, always procrastinating and avoiding unpleasant duties, and often reproaching himself in vain; a man, observe, who at *any* time and in *any* circumstances would be unequal to the task assigned to Hamlet. And thus, I must maintain, it degrades Hamlet and travesties the play. For Hamlet, according to all the indications in the text, was not naturally or normally such a man, but rather, I venture to affirm, a man who at any *other* time and in any *other* circumstances than those presented would have been perfectly equal to his task; and it is, in fact, the very cruelty of his fate that the crisis of his life comes on him at the one moment when he cannot meet it, and when his highest gifts, instead of helping him, conspire to paralyse him." Brandes[3] says very

---

[1] Bradley: Shakespearean Tragedy, 2nd Ed., 1905, p. 102.
[2] idem: op. cit., p. 107.
[3] G. Brandes: William Shakespeare, 1898, Vol. II, p. 31.

pointedly: "Shakespeare is misunderstood when Hamlet is taken for that modern product—a mind diseased by morbid reflection, without capacity for action. It is nothing less than a freak of ironic fate that *he* should have become a sort of symbol of reflective sloth, this man who has gunpowder in every nerve, and all the dynamite of genius in his nature".

In the second place, as will later be expounded, Hamlet's attitude is never that of a man who feels himself not equal to the task, but rather that of a man who for some reason cannot bring himself to perform his plain duty. The whole picture is not, as Goethe depicted, one of a gentle soul crushed beneath a colossal task, but one of a strong man tortured by some mysterious inhibition.

Already in 1827 a protest was raised by Hermes[1] against Goethe's interpretation, and since then a number of hypotheses have been put forward in which Hamlet's temperamental deficiencies are made to play a very subordinate part. The *second* of the group of views here discussed goes in fact to the opposite extreme, and finds in the difficulty of the task itself the sole reason for the non-performance of it; it has therefore been termed the "objective", in contrast to the former "subjective" hypothesis. This view was first hinted by Fletcher,[2] perhaps deriving from Hartley Coleridge, and was independently developed by Klein[3] and Werder.[4] It

---

[1] Hermes: Ueber Shakespeare's Hamlet und seine Beurteiler, 1827.

[2] Fletcher: *Westminster Review*, Sept. 1845.

[3] Klein: "Emil Devrient's Hamlet", *Berliner Modenspiegel, eine Zeitschrift für die elegante Welt*, 1846, Nr. 23, 24.

[4] Werder: "Vorlesungen über Shakespeare's Hamlet", *Preussische Jahrbücher* 1873–4; reprinted in book form, 1875. Translated by E. Wilder, 1907, under the title of "The Heart of Hamlet's Mystery".

maintains that the extrinsic difficulties inherent in the task were so stupendous as to have deterred anyone, however determined. To do this it is necessary to conceive the task in a different light from the usual one. As a development largely of the Hegelian teachings on the subject of abstract justice, Klein, and to a lesser extent Werder, contended that the essence of Hamlet's revenge consisted not merely in slaying the murderer, but of convicting him of his crime in the eyes of the nation. The argument, then, runs as follows: The nature of Claudius' crime was so frightful and so unnatural as to render it incredible unless supported by a very considerable body of evidence. If Hamlet had simply slain his uncle, and then proclaimed, without a shred of supporting evidence, that he had done it to avenge a fratricide, the nation would infallibly have cried out upon him, not only for murdering his uncle to seize the throne himself, but also for selfishly seeking to cast an infamous slur on the memory of a man who could no longer defend his honour. This would have resulted in the sanctification of the uncle, and so the frustration of the revenge. In other words, it was the difficulty not so much of the act itself that deterred Hamlet as of the situation that would necessarily result from the act.

Thanks mainly to Werder's forcible presentation of this view, several prominent authors, including Furness,[1] Halliwell-Phillips,[2] Widgery,[3] Hudson,[4] Corson,[5] Dam-

---

[1] Furness: A New Variorum Edition of Shakespeare, Vols. III and IV, 1877.

[2] Halliwell-Phillips: Memoranda on the Tragedy of Hamlet, 1879.

[3] W. H. Widgery: Harness Prize Essays on the First Quarto of Hamlet, 1880.

[4] Hudson: Shakespeare's Life, Art, and Characters, 2nd Ed., 1882.

[5] H. Corson: "Hamlet", *Shakesperiana*, 1886.

me,[1] Alice Brotherton,[2] Traut,[3] and Rolfe,[4] have given it their adherence: Werder himself confidently wrote of his thesis: "That this point for a century long should never have been seen is the most incomprehensible thing that has ever happened in aesthetic criticism from the very beginning of its existence". It has not, however, found much favour in the Hamlet literature proper, and has been crushingly refuted by a number of able critics, more particularly by Hebler,[5] Baumgart,[6] Bulthaupt,[7] Ribbeck,[8] Loening,[9] Bradley,[10] Tolman,[11] and Robertson.[12]

I need, therefore, do no more than mention one or two of the objections that can be raised to it. It will be seen that to support this hypothesis the task has in two respects to be made to appear more difficult than it really is: first, it is assumed to be not a simple revenge in the ordinary sense of the word, but a complicated bringing to judgement in a more or less legal way; and secondly, the importance of the external obstacles has to be greatly exaggerated. This distortion of the meaning of the revenge is purely gratuitous and has no warrant

[1] Damme: "Warum zaudert Hamlet?", *Preussische Jahrbücher*, Sept. 1890. S. 250 et seq.

[2] Alice Brotherton: "The Real Hamlet and the Hamlet Oldest of All", *Poet-Lore*, 1905, Vol. XVI, p. 110.

[3] H. Traut: Die Hamlet Kontroverse im Umrisse bearbeitet, 1898.

[4] Rolfe: Introduction to the English Translation of Werder, op. cit., 1907.

[5] Hebler: Aufsätze über Shakespeare, 2. Ausg., 1874, S. 258–78.

[6] Baumgart: Die Hamlet-Tragödie und ihre Kritik, 1877, S. 7–29.

[7] Bulthaupt: Dramaturgie des Schauspiels, 4. Aufl. 1891, II. S. 237.

[8] Ribbeck: Hamlet und seine Ausleger, 1891, S. 567.

[9] Loening: op. cit., S. 110–13 and 220–4.

[10] Bradley: op. cit., Art. "Hamlet".

[11] Tolman: Views about Hamlet and other Essays, 1904.

[12] J. M. Robertson: The Problem of "Hamlet", 1919, pp. 21–3.

in any passage of the play, nor elsewhere where the word is used in Shakespeare.[1] Hamlet never doubted that he was the legitimately appointed instrument of punishment, and when at the end of the play he secures his revenge the dramatic situation is correctly resolved, although the nation is not even informed, let alone convinced, of the murder that is being avenged. To secure evidence that would convict the uncle in a court of law was from the nature of the case impossible, and no tragical situation can arise from an attempt to achieve what is evidently impossible, nor could the interest of the spectator be aroused for an obviously one-sided struggle.

The external situation is similarly distorted for the needs of this hypothesis. On which side the people would have been in any conflict is clearly enough perceived by Claudius, who dare not even punish Hamlet for killing Polonius (Act IV, Sc. 3):

> Yet must not we put the strong law on him;
> He's loved of the distracted multitude,
> Who like not in their judgment, but their eyes;

and again in Act IV, Sc. 7,

>   The other motive,
> Why to a public count I might not go,
> Is the great love the general gender bear him,
> Who dipping all his faults in their affection,
> Would like the spring that turneth wood to stone,
> Convert his gyves to graces so that my arrows,
> Too lightly timber'd for so loud a wind,
> Would have reverted to my bow again,
> And not where I had aim'd them.

[1] Loening (op. cit., Cap. VI) has made a detailed study of the significance of revenge in Shakespeare's period and as illustrated throughout his works; his conclusion on the point admits of no questioning.

The ease with which the people could be roused against Claudius is well demonstrated after Polonius's death, when Laertes carried them with him in an irresistible demand for vengeance, which would promptly have been consummated had not the king immediately succeeded in convincing the avenger that he was innocent. Here the people, the false Danish dogs whose loyalty to Claudius was so feather-light that they gladly hailed as king even Laertes, a man who had no sort of claim on the throne, were ready enough to believe in the murderous guilt of their monarch without any shred of supporting evidence, when the accusation was not even true, and where no motive for murder could be discerned at all approaching in weight the two powerful ones that had actually led him to kill his brother. Where Laertes succeeded, it is not likely that Hamlet, the darling of the people, would have failed. Can we not imagine the march of events during the play before the court, had Hamlet there shown the same mettle as Laertes did: the straining observation of the forewarned nobles, the starting up of the guilty monarch who can bear the spectacle no longer, the open murmuring of the audience, the resistless impeachment by the avenger, and the instant execution effected by him and his devoted friends? Indeed, the whole Laertes episode seems almost deliberately to have been woven into the drama so as to show the world how a pious son should really deal with his father's murderer, how possible was the vengeance in just these particular circumstances, and by contrast to illuminate the ignoble vacillation of Hamlet, whose honour had been doubly wounded by the same treacherous villain.[1]

---

[1] Note to what fine details this contrast is painted. When Claudius asks Laertes:

The deeper meaning of the difference in the behaviour of the two men in a similar situation has been aptly pointed out by Storfer:[1] "When we compare the earlier versions of the Hamlet theme with Shakespeare's tragedy, Shakespeare's great psychological intuition becomes evident. The earlier versions turned on a political action relating to the State: the heir to the throne wreaks vengeance on the usurper for the murder of the king. In Shakespeare the family tragedy is placed in the foreground. The origin of all revolutions is the revolution in the family. Shakespeare's Hamlet is too philosophical a man, too much given to introspection, not to feel the personal and family motive behind the general political undertaking. Laertes, on the other hand, is blind and deaf to this etymology of feeling, to the unconscious mind; his response to his father Polonius' murder is a political revolt. The behaviour of the two men whose fathers had been murdered well characterizes the conscious and the unconscious mind in the psychology of the revolutionary and of the political criminal."

Most convincing proof of all that the tragedy cannot be interpreted as residing in difficulties produced by the external situation is Hamlet's own attitude towards his task. He never behaves as a man confronted with a straightforward task, in which there are merely external difficulties to overcome. If this had been so surely he would from the first have confided in Horatio and his

---

What would you undertake
To show yourself your father's son in deed
More than in words?

swift comes the ruthless reply:

To cut his throat in th' church.

How different from Hamlet's behaviour in the prayer scene!

[1] Storfer: Zur Sonderstellung des Vatermordes, 1911, S. 14.

other friends who so implicitly believed in him, as he did in the pre-Shakespearean versions of the play when there really were external difficulties of a more serious nature than in Shakespeare's, and would deliberately have set to work with them to formulate plans by means of which these obstacles might be overcome. Instead of this he never makes any serious attempt to deal with the external situation, and indeed throughout the play makes no concrete reference to it as such, even in the significant prayer scene when he had every opportunity to disclose to us the real reason for his continued non-action. There is therefore no escape from the conclusion that so far as the external situation is concerned the task was a possible one, and was regarded as such by Hamlet.

If Hamlet is a man capable of action, and the task one capable of achievement, what then can be the reason that he does not execute it? Critics who have realized the inadequacy of the hypotheses mentioned above—and this is true of nearly all modern critics—have been hard pressed to answer this question. Some, struck by Klein's suggestion that the task is not really what in the play it is said to be, have offered novel interpretations of it. Thus Mauerhof[1] maintains that the Ghost's command to Hamlet was not, as is generally supposed, to avenge his father by killing the King, but merely to put an end to the life of depravity his mother was still leading, and that Hamlet's problem was how to accomplish this without tarnishing her name by disclosing the truth. Dietrich[2] put forward the singular view that Hamlet's task was to restore to Fortinbras the lands that had been unjustly filched from the latter's father. When straits

[1] Mauerhof: Ueber Hamlet, 1882. Reprinted in Shakespeare-Probleme, 1905.

[2] Dietrich: Hamlet, der Konstabel der Vorsehung; eine Shakespeare-Studie, 1883.

such as these are reached it is little wonder that many competent critics have taken refuge in the conclusion that the tragedy is in its essence inexplicable, incoherent, and incongruous. This view, first critically sustained by Rapp in 1846,[1] has been developed by a number of writers, including von Friefen,[2] Rümelin,[3] Benedix,[4] and many others. The causes of the dramatic imperfection of the play have been variously given: by Dowden[5] as a conscious interpolation by Shakespeare of some secret, by Reichel[6] as the defacement by an uneducated actor called Shakspere, of a play by an unknown poet called Shakespeare, and so on.

The argument, however, has usually taken the form of direct criticism of the poet's capacity, and therefore is found chiefly among writers of the eighteenth century, such as Hanmer[7] and Mackenzie,[8] i.e. a time before bardolatry had developed, or else at the time when this reached its acme, during the tercentenary of 1864, by authors who headed the revulsion against it, including Von Friefen, Rümelin, and Benedix; the last-named of these ascribes Hamlet's delay solely to the number of wholly superfluous episodes which occupy time in the play. Thirty years ago it was independently revived in a weightier form by three authors, Stoll,[9] Schücking,[10] and particularly J. M. Robertson, basing himself on the recent discoveries concerning the sources of the play.

[1] Rapp: Shakespeare's Schauspiele übersetzt und erläutert, Bd. VIII, 1846.
[2] Von Friefen: Briefe über Shakespeare's Hamlet, 1864.
[3] Rümelin: Shakespeare-Studien, 1886.
[4] Benedix: Die Shakespereomanie, 1873.
[5] Dowden: Shakespeare; his development in his works, 1875.
[6] Reichel: Shakespeare-Litteratur, 1887.
[7] Hanmer: Some Remarks on the Tragedy of Hamlet, 1736.
[8] Mackenzie: op. cit.
[9] Stoll: op. cit.
[10] Schücking: Character Problems in Shakespeare's Plays, 1922.

They created some stir by proclaiming that "Hamlet"
was a botched work of art because Shakespeare had failed
to harmonize the crudities of the original story with his
own more spiritual aims; the old story refused to be
remodelled and hence the various inconsistencies in the
play. Robertson's thesis is that Shakespeare, finding in
the old play "an action that to his time-discounting sense
was one of unexplained delay, elaborated that aspect of
the hero as he did every other",[1] "finally missing artistic
consistency simply because consistency was absolutely
excluded by the material";[2] he concludes that "Hamlet"
is "not finally an intelligible drama as it stands",[3] that
"the play cannot be explained from within",[4] and that
"no jugglery can do away with the fact that the con-
struction is incoherent, and the hero perforce an enigma,
the snare of idolatrous criticism".[5] Bradby,[6] it is true,
grants that Shakespeare could have got the play right
had he taken more trouble. He calls it "one of the greatest
of plays, but not what it has been so often called, a perfect
work of art. Had Shakespeare had the time and inclination he could have made of 'Hamlet' a perfect work of
art". But the others will have none of this. Stoll says there
is no tragic failure, as commonly supposed, in the person
of Hamlet, but the plot and the character are discordant.
Shore maintains that the character is badly drawn, and
that "Shakespeare had no clear idea himself of what he
meant Hamlet to be".[7] No less a person than T. S. Eliot[8]
has adopted the same pessimistic opinion. His terse
summary[9] is that "so far from being Shakespeare's

[1] Robertson: op. cit., p. 18.   [2] idem: op. cit., p. 85.
[3] idem: op. cit., p. 27.   [4] idem: op. cit., p. 29.
[5] idem: op. cit., p. 67.   [6] Bradby: op. cit., p. 59.
[7] W. T. Shore: Shakespeare's Self, 1920, p. 146.
[8] T. S. Eliot: The Sacred Wood, 1920, p. 90. Reprinted in
Selected Essays, 1932.   [9] idem: op. cit., p. 98.

masterpiece, the play is most certainly an artistic failure.
. . . Shakespeare tackled a problem that was too much
for him". A tragedy concerned with excessive reaction to
a guilty mother could not be combined with the intract-
able (revenge) material of the old play.

These adverse opinions of the play have been adequately dealt with by Dover Wilson[1] on the literary
and historical plane, where it becomes the mere psychologist to be silent, and elsewhere he asserts:[2] "The
more one contemplates it the more flawless and subtle
does its technique appear". One may perhaps be allowed
to suggest that the important literary and historical
criteria can be supplemented by a psychological one.
Where the traits and reactions of a character prove to be
harmonious, consistent, and intelligible when examined
in the different layers of the mind, the surface ones
tallying with those of the depths, this consideration may
well be added to others in determining what is a "perfect
work of art". "Hamlet" in my opinion passes this test
however stringently it be applied.

Dover Wilson, however, while maintaining that both
the personality and plot in "Hamlet" are consistent,
nevertheless regards the delay as an inexplicable part of
Hamlet's character: "it puzzles Hamlet, it puzzles us,
and it was *meant* to puzzle us", and again:[3] "We were
never intended to reach the heart of the mystery. That
it has a heart is an illusion; the mystery itself is an
illusion; Hamlet is an illusion". For him[4] this supreme
illusion is the triumph of Shakespeare's unrivalled
dramatic technique. Boas[5] asks: "How can outsiders

[1] Dover Wilson: Hamlet, op. cit., p. xlvii.
[2] idem: What happens in "Hamlet", 1935, p. 237.
[3] idem: Six Tragedies of Shakespeare, 1929, p. 75.
[4] idem: "What Happens in 'Hamlet' ", op. cit., p. 229.
[5] Boas: loc. cit.

grasp the secret of a life that was a mystery to the man who lived it?"

To deny the possibility of a solution, or even the real existence of the problem, has always been the last resort when faced with an apparently insoluble enigma. Many upholders of this negative conclusion have consoled themselves with the thought that in this very obscurity, so characteristic of life in general, lie the power and attractiveness of the play. Even Grillparzer[1] saw in its impenetrability the reason for its colossal effectiveness; he adds, "It becomes thereby a true picture of universal happenings and produces the same sense of immensity as these do". Now vagueness and obfuscation may or may not be characteristic of life in general, but they are certainly not the attributes of a successful drama. No disconnected and intrinsically meaningless drama could have produced the effect on its audiences that "Hamlet" has continuously done for the past three centuries. The underlying meaning of its main theme may be obscure, but that there is one, and one which touches matters of vital interest to the human heart, is empirically demonstrated by the uniform success with which the drama appeals to the most diverse audiences. To hold the contrary is to deny all the accepted canons of dramatic art: "Hamlet" as a masterpiece stands or falls by these canons.

[1] Grillparzer: Studien zur Litterärgeschichte, 3. Ausgabe, 1880.

CHAPTER III

THE PSYCHO-ANALYTICAL SOLUTION

WE ARE compelled then to take the position that there is some cause for Hamlet's vacillation which has not yet been fathomed. If this lies neither in his incapacity for action in general, nor in the inordinate difficulty of the particular task in question, then it must of necessity lie in the third possibility—namely, in some special feature of the task that renders it repugnant to him. This conclusion, that Hamlet at heart does not want to carry out the task, seems so obvious that it is hard to see how any open-minded reader of the play could avoid making it.[1] Some of the direct evidence for it furnished in the play will presently be brought forward when we discuss the problem of the cause of the repugnance, but it will first be necessary to mention some of the views that have been expressed on the subject.

The first writer clearly to recognize that Hamlet was a man not baffled in his endeavours but struggling in an internal conflict was Ulrici,[2] in 1839. The details of Ulrici's hypothesis, which like Klein's originated in the Hegelian views of morality, are not easy to follow, but the essence of it is the contention that Hamlet gravely doubted the moral legitimacy of revenge. He was thus plunged into a struggle between his natural tendency to

[1] Anyone who doubts this conclusion is recommended to read Loening's convincing chapter (XII), "Hamlet's Verhalten gegen seine Aufgabe".

[2] Ulrici: Shakespeare's dramatische Kunst; Geschichte und Charakteristik des Shakespeare'schen Dramas, 1839.

avenge his father and his highly developed ethical and Christian views, which forbade the indulging of this instinctive desire. This hypothesis has been further developed on moral, ethical, and religious planes by Tolman,[1] Arndt,[2] Egan,[3] Wright,[4] Liebau,[5] Mézières,[6] Gerth,[7] Baumgart,[8] Robertson,[9] and Ford.[10] Von Berger [11] says that the task laid on him is beneath Hamlet's dignity: "He is too wise and too noble for this pernicious world". Foss[12] thinks that the motive for Hamlet's delay is to gain time so as to think out how he can sinlessly commit a great sin; his conscience tells him it was wrong even to think of assassination, and that what he should do was to denounce Claudius. Kohler[13] ingeniously transferred the conflict to the sphere of jurisprudence, maintaining that Hamlet represented a type in advance of his time in recognizing the superiority of legal punishment over private revenge or family vendetta and was thus a fighter in the van of progress; he writes:[14] "Hamlet is a corner-stone in the

[1] Tolman: "A View of the Views about 'Hamlet' ", *Publications of the Modern Language Association of America*, 1898, p. 155.
[2] Wilhelm Arndt: "Hamlet, der Christ", *Die Zukunft*, 1896, S. 275.
[3] M. F. Egan: "The Puzzle of Hamlet" in The Ghost in Hamlet and Other Essays, 1906.
[4] W. B. Wright: "Hamlet", *Atlantic Monthly*, 1902, p. 686.
[5] Liebau: Studien über William Shakespeares Trauerspiel Hamlet. Date not stated.
[6] Mézières: Shakespeare, ses oeuvres et ses critiques, 1860.
[7] Gerth: op. cit.
[8] Baumgart: op. cit.
[9] J. M. Robertson: Montaigne and Shakspere, 1897, p. 129.
[10] Ford: Shakespeare's Hamlet: A New Theory, 1900.
[11] A. von Berger: "Hamlet" in Dramaturgische Vorträge, 1890.
[12] G. R. Foss: What the Author Meant, 1932, p. 13.
[13] Kohler: Shakespeare vor dem Forum der Jurisprudenz, 1883; and Zur Lehre von der Blutrache, 1885. See also *Zeitschrift für vergleichende Rechtswissenschaft*, Bd. V, S. 330.
[14] Kohler: Shakespeare etc.; op. cit., S. 189.

evolution of law and morality". A similar view has been developed by Rubinstein.[1] This special pleading has been effectually refuted by Loening[2] and Fuld;[3] it is contradicted by all historical considerations. Finally, Schipper,[4] Gelber,[5] and, more recently, Stoll[6] have suggested that the conflict was a purely intellectual one, Hamlet being unable to satisfy himself of the adequacy or reliability of the Ghost's evidence. In his interesting work Figgis combines these views by insisting that the play is a tragedy of honour, Hamlet's main instinct: "In striking at the King without a full assurance of his guilt, was to him not only to strike at the legal monarch of the realm, but also to seem as though he was seizing a pretext to strike for the throne, he being the next in succession":[7] "What seems like indecision in the early portion of the play is really the honourable desire not to let his mere hatred of the King prick him into a capital action against an innocent man, to prove that the apparition of his father was no heated fantasy, and, above all, not to take action till he was assured that his action would not involve his mother".[8]

The obvious question that one puts to the upholders of any of the hypotheses just mentioned is: why did Hamlet in his monologues give us no indication whatsoever of the nature of the conflict in his mind? As we shall presently

[1] Rubinstein: Hamlet als Neurastheniker, 1896.

[2] Loening: *Zeitschrift für die gesamte Strafrechtswissenschaft*, Bd. V, S. 191.

[3] Fuld: "Shakespeare und die Blutrache", *Dramaturgische Blätter und Bühnen-Rundschau*, 1888, Nr. 44.

[4] Schipper: Shakespeare's Hamlet; ästhetische Erläuterung des Hamlet, 1862.

[5] Gelber: Shakespeare'sche Probleme, Plan und Einheit im Hamlet, 1891.

[6] Stoll: op. cit. (1919).

[7] Figgis: op. cit., p. 213.

[8] idem: op. cit., p. 232.

note, he gave several pretended excuses for his hesitancy, but never once did he hint at any doubt about what his duty was in the matter. He was always clear enough about what he *ought* to do; the conflict in his mind ranged about the question why he couldn't bring himself to do it. If Hamlet had at any time been asked whether it was right for him to kill his uncle, or whether he really intended to do so, no one can seriously doubt what his instant answer would have been. Throughout the play we see his mind irrevocably made up on the desirability of a given course of action, which he fully accepts as being his bounden duty; indeed, he would have resented the mere insinuation of doubt on this point as an untrue slur on his filial piety. Ulrici, Baumgart, and Kohler try to meet this difficulty by assuming that the ethical objection to personal revenge was never clearly present to Hamlet's mind; it was a deep and undeveloped feeling which had not fully dawned. I would agree that only in some such way as this can the difficulty be logically met, and further that in recognizing Hamlet's non-consciousness of the cause of his repugnance to his task we are nearing the core of the mystery. In fact Hamlet tells us so himself in so many words (in his bitter cry—Act IV, Sc. 3—*I do not know why*, etc.). But an insurmountable obstacle in the way of accepting any of the causes of repugnance suggested above is that the nature of them is such that a keen and introspective thinker, as Hamlet was, would infallibly have recognized some indication of their presence, and would have openly debated them instead of deceiving himself with a number of false pretexts in the way we shall presently recall. Loening[1] well states this in the sentence: "If it had been a question of a conflict between the duty of revenge imposed from

---

[1] Loening: Die Hamlet-Tragödie Shakespeares, 1893, S. 78.

without and an inner *moral* or *juristic* counter-impulse, this discord and its cause *must* have been brought into the region of reflection in a man so capable of thought, and so accustomed to it, as Hamlet was".

In spite of this difficulty the hint of an approaching solution encourages us to pursue more closely the argument at that point. The hypothesis just stated may be correct up to a certain stage and then have failed for lack of special knowledge to guide it further. Thus Hamlet's hesitancy may have been due to an internal conflict between the impulse to fulfil his task on the one hand and some special cause of repugnance to it on the other; further, the explanation of his not disclosing this cause of repugnance may be that he was not conscious of its nature; and yet the cause may be one that doesn't happen to have been considered by any of the upholders of this hypothesis. In other words, the first two stages in the argument may be correct, but not the third. This is the view that will now be developed, but before dealing with the third stage of the argument it is first necessary to establish the probability of the first two—namely, that Hamlet's hesitancy was due to some special cause of repugnance for his task and that he was unaware of the nature of this repugnance.

A preliminary obstruction to this line of thought, based on some common prejudices on the subject of mental dynamics, may first be considered. If Hamlet was not aware of the nature of his inhibition, doubt may be felt concerning the possibility of our penetrating to it. This pessimistic thought was expressed by Baumgart[1] as follows: "What hinders Hamlet in his revenge is for him himself a problem and *therefore* it must remain a problem for us all". Fortunately for our investigation,

[1] Baumgart: op. cit., S. 48.

however, psycho-analytic studies have demonstrated beyond doubt that mental trends hidden from the subject himself may come to external expression in ways that reveal their nature to a trained observer, so that the possibility of success is not to be thus excluded. Loening[1] has further objected to this hypothesis that the poet himself has not disclosed this hidden mental trend, or even given any indication of it. The first part of his objection is certainly true—otherwise there would be no problem to discuss, but we shall presently see that the second is by no means true. It may be asked: why has the poet not put in a clearer light the mental trend we are trying to discover? Strange as it may appear, the answer is probably the same as with Hamlet himself— namely, he could not because he was unaware of its nature. We shall later deal with this question in connection with the relation of the poet to the play.

As Trench well says:[2] "We find it hard, with Shakespeare's help, to understand Hamlet: even Shakespeare, perhaps, found it hard to understand him: Hamlet himself finds it impossible to understand himself. Better able than other men to read the hearts and motives of others, he is yet quite unable to read his own". I know of no more authentic statement than this in the whole literature on the Hamlet problem. But, if the motive of the play is so obscure, to what can we attribute its powerful effect on the audience, since, as Kohler[3] asks, "Who has ever seen Hamlet and not felt the fearful conflict that moves the soul of the hero?" This can only be because the hero's conflict finds its echo in a similar inner conflict in the mind of the hearer, and the more intense is this

---

[1] Loening: op. cit., S. 78, 79.   [2] Trench: op. cit., p. 115.
[3] Kohler: Shakespeare vor dem Forum der Jurisprudenz, 1883, S. 195.

already present conflict the greater is the effect of the drama.[1] Again, it is certain that the hearer himself does not know the inner cause of the conflict in his own mind, but experiences only the outer manifestations of it. So we reach the apparent paradox that the hero, the poet, and the audience are all profoundly moved by feelings due to a conflict of the source of which they are unaware.

The fact, however, that such a conclusion should appear paradoxical is in itself a censure on popular ignorance of the actual workings of the human mind, and before undertaking to sustain the assertions made in the preceding paragraph it will first be necessary to make a few observations on the prevailing views of motive and conduct in general. The new science of clinical psychology stands nowhere in sharper contrast to the older attitudes towards mental functioning than on this very matter. Whereas the generally accepted view of man's mind, usually implicit and frequently explicit in psychological writings and elsewhere, regards it as an interplay of various processes that are for the most part known to the subject, or are at all events accessible to careful introspection on his part, the analytic methods of clinical psychology have on the contrary decisively proved that a far greater number of these processes than is commonly surmised arises from origins that he never even suspects. Man's belief that he is a self-conscious animal, alive to the desires that impel or inhibit his actions, is the last stronghold of that anthropomorphic and anthropocentric outlook on life which has so long dominated his philosophy, his theology, and, above all, his psychology.

---

[1] It need hardly be said that the play, like most others, appeals to its audience in a number of different respects. We are here considering only the main appeal, the central conflict in the tragedy.

In other words, the tendency to take man at his own valuation is rarely resisted, and we assume that the surest way of finding out why a person commits a given act is simply to ask him, relying on the knowledge that he, as we ourselves would in a like circumstance, will feel certain of the answer and will almost infallibly provide a plausible reason for his conduct. Special objective methods of penetrating into the more obscure mental processes, however, disclose the most formidable obstacles in the way of this direct introspective route, and reveal powers of self-deception in the human mind to which a limit has yet to be found. If I may quote from a former paper:[1] "We are beginning to see man not as the smooth, self-acting agent he pretends to be, but as he really is, a creature only dimly conscious of the various influences that mould his thought and action, and blindly resisting with all the means at his command the forces that are making for a higher and fuller consciousness".

That Hamlet is suffering from an internal conflict the essential nature of which is inaccessible to his introspection is evidenced by the following considerations. Throughout the play we have the clearest picture of a man who sees his duty plain before him, but who shirks it at every opportunity and suffers in consequence the most intense remorse. To paraphrase Sir James Paget's well-known description of hysterical paralysis: Hamlet's advocates say he cannot do his duty, his detractors say he will not, whereas the truth is that he cannot will. Further than this, the deficient will-power is localized to the one question of killing his uncle; it is what may be termed a *specific aboulia*. Now instances of such specific aboulias in real life invariably prove, when analysed, to

[1] "Rationalization in Every Day Life", *Journal of Abnormal Psychology*, 1908, p. 168.

be due to an unconscious repulsion against the act that cannot be performed (or else against something closely associated with the act, so that the idea of the act becomes also involved in the repulsion). In other words, whenever a person cannot bring himself to do something that every conscious consideration tells him he should do—and which he may have the strongest conscious desire to do—it is always because there is some hidden reason why a part of him doesn't want to do it; this reason he will not own to himself and is only dimly if at all aware of. That is exactly the case with Hamlet. Time and again he works himself up, points out to himself his obvious duty, with the cruellest self-reproaches lashes himself to agonies of remorse—and once more falls away into inaction. He eagerly seizes at every excuse for occupying himself with any other matter than the performance of his duty—even in the last scene of the last act entering on the distraction of a quite irrelevant fencing-match with a man who he must know wants to kill him, an eventuality that would put an end to all hope of fulfilling his task: just as on a lesser plane a person faced with a distasteful task, e.g. writing a difficult letter, will whittle away his time in arranging, tidying, and fidgeting with any little occupation that may serve as a pretext for procrastination. Bradley[1] even goes so far as to make out a case for the view that Hamlet's self-accusation of "bestial oblivion" is to be taken in a literal sense, his unconscious detestation of his task being so intense as to enable him actually to forget it for periods.

Highly significant is the fact that the grounds Hamlet gives for his hesitancy are grounds none of which will stand any serious consideration, and which continually change from one time to another. One moment he pre-

[1] Bradley: op. cit., pp. 125, 126, 410, 411.

tends he is too cowardly to perform the deed, at another he questions the truthfulness of the ghost, at another—when the opportunity presents itself in its naked form—he thinks the time is unsuited, it would be better to wait till the King was at some evil act and then to kill him, and so on. They have each of them, it is true, a certain plausibility—so much so that some writers have accepted them at face value; but surely no pretext would be of any use if it were not plausible. As Madariaga[1] truly says: "The argument that the reasons given by Hamlet not to kill the king at prayers are cogent is irrelevant. For the man who wants to procrastinate cogent arguments are more valuable than mere pretexts". Take, for instance, the matter of the credibility of the ghost. There exists an extensive and very interesting literature concerning Elizabethan beliefs in supernatural visitation. It was doubtless a burning topic, a focal point of the controversies about the conflicting theologies of the age, and moreover, affecting the practical question of how to treat witches. But there is no evidence of Hamlet (or Shakespeare!) being specially interested in theology, and from the moment when the ghost confirms the slumbering suspicion in his mind ("O, my prophetic soul! My uncle!") his intuition must indubitably have convinced him of the ghost's veridical nature. He never really doubted the villainy of his uncle.

When a man gives at different times a different reason for his conduct it is safe to infer that, whether consciously or not, he is concealing the true reason. Wetz,[2] discussing a similar problem in reference to Iago, truly observes: "Nothing proves so well how false are the motives with

[1] Madariaga: op. cit., p. 98.
[2] Wetz: Shakespeare vom Standpunkt der vergleichenden Litteraturgeschichte, 1890, Bd. I, S. 186.

which Iago tries to persuade himself as *the constant change in these motives*". We can therefore safely dismiss all the alleged motives that Hamlet propounds, as being more or less successful attempts on his part to blind himself with self-deception. Loening's[1] summing-up of them is not too emphatic when he says: "They are all mutually contradictory; *they are one and all false pretexts*". The alleged motives excellently illustrate the psychological mechanisms of evasion and rationalization I have elsewhere described.[2] It is not necessary, however, to discuss them here individually, for Loening has with the greatest perspicacity done this in full detail and has effectually demonstrated how utterly untenable they all are.[3]

Still, in his moments of self-reproach Hamlet sees clearly enough the recalcitrancy of his conduct and renews his efforts to achieve action. It is noticeable how his outbursts of remorse are evoked by external happenings which bring back to his mind that which he would so gladly forget, and which, according to Bradley, he does at times forget: particularly effective in this respect are incidents that contrast with his own conduct, as when the player is so moved over the fate of Hecuba (Act II, Sc. 2), or when Fortinbras takes the field and "finds quarrel in a straw when honour's at the stake" (Act IV, Sc. 4). On the former occasion, stung by the monstrous way in which the player pours out his feeling at the thought of Hecuba, he arraigns himself in words which surely should effectually dispose of the view that he has any doubt where his duty lies.

What's Hecuba to him, or he to Hecuba,
That he should weep for her? What would he do,

[1] Loening: op. cit., S. 245.   [2] op. cit., p. 161.
[3] See especially his analysis of Hamlet's pretext for non-action in the prayer scene: op. cit., S. 240–2.

Had he the motive and the cue for passion
That I have? He would drown the stage with tears
And cleave the general ear with horrid speech,
Make mad the guilty and appal the free,
Confound the ignorant, and amaze indeed
The very faculties of eyes and ears; yet I,
A dull and muddy-mettled rascal, peak
Like John-a-dreams, unpregnant of my cause,[1]
And can say nothing; no, not for a king,
Upon whose property and most dear life
A damn'd defeat was made: Am I a coward?
Who calls me villain, breaks my pate across,
Plucks off my beard and blows it in my face,
Tweaks me by the nose, gives me the lie i' the throat
As deep as to the lungs? Who does me this?
Ha, 'swounds, I should take it: for it cannot be
But I am pigeon-liver'd, and lack gall
To make oppression bitter, or ere this
I should ha' fatted all the region kites
With this slave's offal. Bloody, bawdy villain!
Remorseless, treacherous, lecherous, kindless villain!
O, vengeance!
Why, what an ass am I! This is most brave,
That I, the son of a dear father murder'd,
Prompted to my revenge by heaven and hell,
Must like a whore unpack my heart with words,
And fall a-cursing like a very drab;
A scullion![2]

The readiness with which his guilty conscience is
stirred into activity is again evidenced on the second
appearance of the Ghost, when Hamlet cries,

---

[1] How the essence of the situation is conveyed in these four
words.

[2] Dover Wilson considers this a misprint for "stallion".

Do you not come your tardy son to chide,
That lapsed in time and passion lets go by
Th'important acting of your dread command?
O, say!

The Ghost at once confirms this misgiving by answering,

Do not forget! this visitation
Is but to whet thy almost blunted purpose.

In short, the whole picture presented by Hamlet, his deep depression, the hopeless note in his attitude towards the world and towards the value of life, his dread of death,[1] his repeated reference to bad dreams, his self-accusations, his desperate efforts to get away from the thoughts of his duty, and his vain attempts to find an excuse for his procrastination: all this unequivocally points to a *tortured conscience*, to some hidden ground for shirking his task, a ground which he dare not or cannot avow to himself. We have, therefore, to take up the argument again at this point, and to seek for some evidence that may serve to bring to light the hidden counter-motive.

The extensive experience of the psycho-analytic researches carried out by Freud and his school during the past half-century has amply demonstrated that certain kinds of mental process show a greater tendency to

---

[1] Tieck (Dramaturgische Blätter, II, 1826) saw in Hamlet's cowardly fear of death a chief reason for his hesitancy in executing his vengeance. How well Shakespeare understood what this fear was like may be inferred from Claudio's words in "Measure for Measure":

> The weariest and most loathed worldly life
> That age, ache, penury and imprisonment
> Can lay on nature is a paradise
> To what we fear of death.

be inaccessible to consciousness (put technically, to be "repressed") than others. In other words, it is harder for a person to realize the existence in his mind of some mental trends than it is of others. In order therefore to gain a proper perspective it is necessary briefly to inquire into the relative frequency with which various sets of mental processes are "repressed". Experience shows that this can be correlated with the degree of compatibility of these various sets with the ideals and standards accepted by the conscious ego; the less compatible they are with these the more likely are they to be "repressed". As the standards acceptable to consciousness are in considerable measure derived from the immediate environment, one may formulate the following generalization: those processes are most likely to be "repressed" by the individual which are most disapproved of by the particular circle of society to whose influence he has chiefly been subjected during the period when his character was being formed. Biologically stated, this law would run: "That which is unacceptable to the herd becomes unacceptable to the individual member", it being understood that the term herd is intended here in the sense of the particular circle defined above, which is by no means necessarily the community at large. It is for this reason that moral, social, ethical, or religious tendencies are seldom "repressed", for, since the individual originally received them from his herd, they can hardly ever come into conflict with the dicta of the latter. This merely says that a man cannot be ashamed of that which he respects; the apparent exceptions to this rule need not be here explained.

The language used in the previous paragraph will have indicated that by the term "repression" we denote an active dynamic process. Thoughts that are "repressed" are actively kept from consciousness by a definite force and with the expenditure of more or less mental effort, though the person concerned is rarely aware of this. Further, what is thus kept from consciousness typically possesses an energy of its own; hence our frequent use of such expressions as "trend", "tendency", etc. A little consideration of the genetic aspects of the matter will make it comprehensible that the trends most likely to be "repressed" are those belonging to what are called the innate impulses, as contrasted with secondarily acquired ones. Loening[1] seems very discerningly to have grasped this, for, in commenting on a remark of Kohler's to the effect that "where a feeling impels us to action or to omission, it is replete with a hundred reasons—with reasons that are as light as soap-bubbles, but which through self-deception appear to us as highly respectable and compelling motives, because they are hugely magnified in the (concave) mirror of our own feeling", he writes: "But this does not hold good, as Kohler and others believe, when we are impelled by *moral* feelings of which reason *approves* (for these we admit to ourselves, they need no excuse), only for feelings that arise from our *natural man*, those the gratification of which is *opposed by our reason*". It only remains to add the obvious corollary that, as the herd unquestionably selects from the "natural" instincts the sexual one on which to lay its heaviest ban, so it is the various psycho-sexual trends that are most often "repressed" by the individual. We have here the explanation of the clinical experience that the more intense and the more obscure is a given case of deep mental conflict the more certainly will it be found on adequate analysis to centre about a sexual problem. On the surface, of course, this does not appear so, for, by

[1] Loening: op. cit., S. 245, 246.

means of various psychological defensive mechanisms, the depression, doubt, despair, and other manifestations of the conflict are transferred on to more tolerable and permissible topics, such as anxiety about worldly success or failure, about immortality and the salvation of the soul, philosophical considerations about the value of life, the future of the world, and so on.

Bearing these considerations in mind, let us return to Hamlet. It should now be evident that the conflict hypotheses discussed above, which see Hamlet's conscious impulse towards revenge inhibited by an unconscious misgiving of a highly ethical kind, are based on ignorance of what actually happens in real life, since misgivings of this order belong in fact to the more conscious layers of the mind rather than to the deeper, unconscious ones. Hamlet's intense self-study would speedily have made him aware of any such misgivings and, although he might subsequently have ignored them, it would almost certainly have been by the aid of some process of rationalization which would have enabled him to deceive himself into believing that they were ill-founded; he would in any case have remained conscious of the nature of them. We have therefore to invert these hypotheses and realize —as his words so often indicate—that the positive striving for vengeance, the pious task laid on him by his father, was to him the moral and social one, the one approved of by his consciousness, and that the "repressed" inhibiting striving against the act of vengeance arose in some hidden source connected with his more personal, natural instincts. The former striving has already been considered, and indeed is manifest in every speech in which Hamlet debates the matter: the second is, from its nature, more obscure and has next to be investigated.

This is perhaps most easily done by inquiring more

intently into Hamlet's precise attitude towards the object
of his vengeance, Claudius, and towards the crimes that
have to be avenged. These are two: Claudius' incest with
the Queen,[1] and his murder of his brother. Now it is of
great importance to note the profound difference in
Hamlet's attitude towards these two crimes. Intellectually
of course he abhors both, but there can be no question
as to which arouses in him the deeper loathing. Whereas
the murder of his father evokes in him indignation and a
plain recognition of his obvious duty to avenge it, his
mother's guilty conduct awakes in him the intensest
horror. Furnivall[2] remarks, in speaking of the Queen,
"Her disgraceful adultery and incest, and treason to his
noble father's memory, Hamlet has felt in his inmost
soul. Compared to their ingrain die, Claudius' murder of
his father—notwithstanding all his protestations—is only
a skin-deep stain".

Now, in trying to define Hamlet's attitude towards
his uncle we have to guard against assuming off-hand
that this is a simple one of mere execration, for there is a
possibility of complexity arising in the following way:
The uncle has not merely committed *each* crime, he has
committed *both* crimes, a distinction of considerable
importance, since the *combination* of crimes allows the
admittance of a new factor, produced by the possible
inter-relation of the two, which may prevent the result
from being simply one of summation. In addition, it has
to be borne in mind that the perpetrator of the crimes is a
relative, and an exceedingly near relative. The possible
inter-relationship of the crimes, and the fact that the
author of them is an actual member of the family,

---

[1] Had this relationship not counted as incestuous, then Queen
Elizabeth would have had no right to the throne; she would have
been a bastard, Katherine of Aragon being still alive at her birth.

[2] Furnivall: Introduction to the "Leopold" Shakespeare, p. 72.

give scope for a confusion in their influence on Hamlet's mind which may be the cause of the very obscurity we are seeking to clarify.

Let us first pursue further the effect on Hamlet of his mother's misconduct. Before he even knows with any certitude, however much he may suspect it, that his father has been murdered he is in the deepest depression, and evidently on account of this misconduct. The connection between the two is unmistakable in the monologue in Act I, Sc. 2, in reference to which Furnivall[1] writes: "One must insist on this, that before any revelation of his father's murder is made to Hamlet, before any burden of revenging that murder is laid upon him, he thinks of suicide as a welcome means of escape from this fair world of God's, made abominable to his diseased and weak imagination by his mother's lust, and the dishonour done by her to his father's memory".

> O that this too too solid[2] flesh would melt,
> Thaw and resolve itself into a dew,
> Or that the Everlasting had not fix'd
> His canon 'gainst self-slaughter, O God, God,
> How weary, stale, flat, and unprofitable
> Seem to me all the uses of this world!
> Fie on 't, O fie, 'tis an unweeded garden
> That grows to seed, things rank and gross in nature
> Possess it merely, that it should come to this,
> But two months dead, nay, not so much, not two,
> So excellent a king; that was to this
> Hyperion to a satyr, so loving to my mother,
> That he might not beteem the winds of heaven

[1] Furnivall: op. cit., p. 70.
[2] Dover Wilson (*Times Literary Supplement*, May 16, 1918) brings forward excellent reasons for thinking that this word is a misprint for "sullied". I use the Shakespearean punctuation he has restored.

Visit her face too roughly—heaven and earth
Must I remember? why, she would hang on him
As if increase of appetite had grown
By what it fed on, and yet within a month,
Let me not think on 't; frailty thy name is woman!
A little month or ere those shoes were old
With which she follow'd my poor father's body
Like Niobe all tears, why she, even she—
O God, a beast that wants discourse of reason
Would have mourn'd longer—married with my uncle,
My father's brother, but no more like my father
Than I to Hercules, within a month,
Ere yet the salt of most unrighteous tears
Had left the flushing in her galled eyes,
She married. O most wicked speed . . . to post
With such dexterity to incestuous sheets!
It is not, nor it cannot come to good,
But break my heart, for I must hold my tongue.

According to Bradley,[1] Hamlet's melancholic disgust
at life was the cause of his aversion from "any kind of
decided action". His explanation of the whole problem
of Hamlet is "the moral shock of the sudden ghastly
disclosure of his mother's true nature",[2] and he regards
the effect of this shock, as depicted in the play, as fully
comprehensible. He says:[3] "Is it possible to conceive an
experience more desolating to a man such as we have
seen Hamlet to be; and is its result anything but perfectly natural? It brings bewildered horror, then loathing, then despair of human nature. His whole mind is
poisoned . . . A nature morally blunter would have
felt even so dreadful a revelation less keenly. A slower and

[1] Bradley: op. cit., p. 122.
[2] idem: op. cit., p. 117.
[3] idem: op. cit., p. 119.

more limited and positive mind might not have extended so widely through the world the disgust and disbelief that have entered it."

But we can rest satisfied with this seemingly adequate explanation of Hamlet's weariness of life only if we accept unquestioningly the conventional standards of the causes of deep emotion. Many years ago Connolly,[1] a well-known psychiatrist, pointed out the disproportion here existing between cause and effect, and gave as his opinion that Hamlet's reaction to his mother's marriage indicated in itself a mental instability, "a predisposition to actual unsoundness"; he writes: "The circumstances are not such as would at once turn a healthy mind to the contemplation of suicide, the last resource of those whose reason has been overwhelmed by calamity and despair." In T. S. Eliot's[2] opinion, also, Hamlet's emotion is in *excess* of the facts as they appear, and he specially contrasts it with Gertrude's negative and insignificant personality. Wihan[3] attributes the exaggerated effect of his misfortunes to Hamlet's "Masslosigkeit" (lack of moderation), which is displayed in every direction. We have unveiled only the exciting cause, not the predisposing cause. The very fact that Hamlet is apparently content with the explanation arouses our misgiving, for, as will presently be expounded, from the very nature of the emotion he cannot be aware of the true cause of it. If we ask, not what ought to produce such soul-paralysing grief and distaste for life, but what in actual fact does produce it, we are compelled to go beyond this explanation and seek for some deeper cause. In real life speedy second marriages occur commonly enough without leading to any such

[1] Connolly: A Study of Hamlet, 1863, pp. 22, 23.
[2] T. S. Eliot: loc. cit.
[3] J. Wihan: "Die Hamletfrage", in Leipziger Beiträge zur englischen Philologie, 1921, S. 89.

result as is here depicted, and when we see them followed by this result we invariably find, if the opportunity for an analysis of the subject's mind presents itself, that there is some other and more hidden reason why the event is followed by this inordinately great effect. The reason always is that the event has awakened to increased activity mental processes that have been "repressed" from the subject's consciousness. His mind has been specially prepared for the catastrophe by previous mental processes with which those directly resulting from the event have entered into association. This is perhaps what Furnivall means when he speaks of the world being made abominable to Hamlet's "diseased imagination". In short, the special nature of the reaction presupposes some special feature in the mental predisposition. Bradley himself has to qualify his hypothesis by inserting the words "to a man such as we have seen Hamlet to be".

We come at this point to the vexed question of Hamlet's sanity, about which so many controversies have raged. Dover Wilson[1] authoritatively writes: "I agree with Loening, Bradley and others that Shakespeare meant us to imagine Hamlet as suffering from some kind of mental disorder throughout the play". The question is what kind of mental disorder and what is its significance dramatically and psychologically. The matter is complicated by Hamlet's frequently displaying simulation (the Antic Disposition),[2] and it has been asked whether this is to conceal his real mental disturbance or cunningly to conceal his purposes in coping with the practical problems of this task? This is a topic that pre-

---

[1] Dover Wilson: What Happens etc., p. 217.
[2] Cp. R. Alexander: "Hamlet, the Classical Malingerer", *Medical Journal and Record*, Sept. 4, 1929, p. 287.

sently will be considered at some length, but there can be few who regard it as a comprehensive statement of Hamlet's mental state. As T. S. Eliot[1] has neatly expressed it, "Hamlet's 'madness' is less than madness and more than feigned".

But what of the mental disorder itself? In the past this little problem in clinical diagnosis seems to have greatly exercised psychiatrists. Some of them, e.g. Thierisch,[2] Sigismund,[3] Stenger,[4] and many others, have simply held that Hamlet was insane, without particularizing the form of insanity. Rosner[5] labelled Hamlet as a hystero-neurasthenic, an opinion contradicted by Rubinstein[6] and Landmann.[7] Most, however, including Kellog,[8] de Boismon,[9] Heuse,[10] Nicholson,[11] and others, have committed themselves to the view that Hamlet was suffering from melancholia, though there are not failing psychiatrists, e.g. Ominus,[12] who reject this. Schücking[13] attributes the delay in his action to Hamlet's being paralysed by melancholia. Laehr[14] has a par-

[1] T. S. Eliot: Selected Essays, 1932, p. 146.

[2] Thierisch: *Nord und Süd*, 1878, Bd. VI.

[3] Sigismund: *Jahrbuch der Deutschen Shakespeare-Gesellschaft*, 1879, Jahrg. XVI.

[4] E. Stenger: Der Hamlet Charakter. Eine psychiatrische Shakespeare-Studie, 1883.

[5] Rosner: Shakespeare's Hamlet im Lichte der Neuropathologie, 1895.   [6] Rubinstein: op. cit.

[7] Landmann: *Zeitschrift für Psychologie*, 1896, Bd. XI.

[8] Kellog: Shakespeare's Delineation of Insanity, 1868.

[9] De Boismon: *Annales médico-psychologiques*, 1868, 4e série, 12e fasc.

[10] Heuse: *Jahrbuch der deutschen Shakespeare-Gesellschaft*, 1876, Jahrg. XIII.

[11] Nicholson: *Transactions of the New Shakespeare Society*, 1880–5, Part II.

[12] Ominus: *Revue des Deux Mondes*, 1876, 3e sér., 14e fasc.

[13] Schücking: Character Problems in Shakespeare's Plays, 1922, p. 162.

[14] Laehr: Die Darstellung krankhafter Geisteszustände in Shakespeare's Dramas, 1898, S. 179, etc.

ticularly ingenious hypothesis which maintains that Shakespeare, having taken over the Ghost episode from the earlier play, was obliged to depict Hamlet as a melancholiac because this was theatrically the most presentable form of insanity in which hallucinations occur. Long ago Dowden made it seem probable that Shakespeare had made use of an important study of melancholia by Timothe Bright,[1] but, although he may have adapted a few phrases to his own use, the clinical picture of Hamlet differs notably from that delineated by Bright.

More to the point is the actual account given in the play by the King, the Queen, Ophelia, and above all, Polonius.[2] In his description, for example, we note—if the Elizabethan language is translated into modern English—the symptoms of dejection, refusal of food, insomnia, crazy behaviour, fits of delirium, and finally of raving madness; Hamlet's poignant parting words to Polonius ("except my life", etc.) cannot mean other than a craving for death. These are undoubtedly suggestive of certain forms of melancholia, and the likeness to manic-depressive insanity, of which melancholia is now known to be but a part, is completed by the occurrence of attacks of great excitement that would nowadays be called "hypomanic", of which Dover Wilson[3] counts no fewer than eight. This modern diagnosis has indeed been suggested, e.g. by Brock,[4] Somerville,[5] and others. Nevertheless, the rapid and startling oscillations between intense excitement and profound depression do not accord with the accepted

[1] Timothe Bright: A Treatise of Melancholia, 1586.
[2] Act 2, Sc. 2. "Fell into a sadness", etc.
[3] Dover Wilson: op. cit., p. 213.
[4] J. H. E. Brock: The Dramatic Purpose of Hamlet, 1935.
[5] H. Somerville: Madness in Shakespearean Tragedy, 1929.

picture of this disorder, and if I had to describe such a condition as Hamlet's in clinical terms—which I am not particularly inclined to—it would have to be as a severe case of hysteria on a cyclothymic basis.

All this, however, is of academic interest only. What we are essentially concerned with is the psychological understanding of the dramatic effect produced by Hamlet's personality and behaviour. That effect would be quite other were the central figure in the play to represent merely a "case of insanity". When that happens, as with Ophelia, such a person passes beyond our ken, is in a sense no more human, whereas Hamlet successfully claims our interest and sympathy to the very end. Shakespeare certainly never intended us to regard Hamlet as insane, so that the "mind o'erthrown" must have some other meaning than its literal one. Robert Bridges[1] has described the matter with exquisite delicacy:

> Hamlet himself would never have been aught to us, or we
> To Hamlet, wer't not for the artful balance whereby
> Shakespeare so gingerly put his sanity in doubt
> Without the while confounding his Reason.

I would suggest that in this Shakespeare's extraordinary powers of observation and penetration granted him a degree of insight that it has taken the world three subsequent centuries to reach. Until our generation (and even now in the juristic sphere) a dividing line separated the sane and responsible from the irresponsible insane. It is now becoming more and more widely recognized that much of mankind lives in an intermediate and unhappy state charged with what Dover Wilson[2] well calls "that sense of frustration, futility and human

[1] Robert Bridges: The Testament of Beauty, I, 577.
[2] Dover Wilson: op. cit., p. 261.

inadequacy which is the burden of the whole symphony" and of which Hamlet is the supreme example in literature. This intermediate plight, in the toils of which perhaps the greater part of mankind struggles and suffers, is given the name of psychoneurosis, and long ago the genius of Shakespeare depicted it for us with faultless insight.

Extensive studies of the past half century, inspired by Freud, have taught us that a psychoneurosis means a state of mind where the person is unduly, and often painfully, driven or thwarted by the "unconscious" part of his mind, that buried part that was once the infant's mind and still lives on side by side with the adult mentality that has developed out of it and should have taken its place. It signifies *internal* mental conflict. We have here the reason why it is impossible to discuss intelligently the state of mind of anyone suffering from a psychoneurosis, whether the description is of a living person or an imagined one, without correlating the manifestations with what must have operated in his infancy and is *still operating*. That is what I propose to attempt here.

For some deep-seated reason, which is to him unacceptable, Hamlet is plunged into anguish at the thought of his father being replaced in his mother's affections by someone else. It is as if his devotion to his mother had made him so jealous for her affection that he had found it hard enough to share this even with his father and could not endure to share it with still another man. Against this thought, however, suggestive as it is, may be urged three objections. First, if it were in itself a full statement of the matter, Hamlet would have been aware of the jealousy, whereas we have concluded that the mental process we are seeking is hidden from him.

Secondly, we see in it no evidence of the arousing of an old and forgotten memory. And, thirdly, Hamlet is being deprived by Claudius of no greater share in the Queen's affection than he had been by his own father, for the two brothers made exactly similar claims in this respect—namely, those of a loved husband. The last-named objection, however, leads us to the heart of the situation. How if, in fact, Hamlet had in years gone by, as a child, bitterly resented having had to share his mother's affection even with his own father, had regarded him as a rival, and had secretly wished him out of the way so that he might enjoy undisputed and undisturbed the monopoly of that affection? If such thoughts had been present in his mind in childhood days they evidently would have been "repressed", and all traces of them obliterated, by filial piety and other educative influences. The actual realization of his early wish in the death of his father at the hands of a jealous rival would then have stimulated into activity these "repressed" memories, which would have produced, in the form of depression and other suffering, an obscure aftermath of his child-hood's conflict. This is at all events the mechanism that is actually found in the real Hamlets who are investigated psychologically.[1]

The explanation, therefore, of the delay and self-frustration exhibited in the endeavour to fulfil his father's demand for vengeance is that to Hamlet the thought of incest and parricide combined is too intolerable to be borne. One part of him tries to carry out the task, the other flinches inexorably from the thought of it. How fain would he blot it out in that "bestial oblivion" which unfortunately for him his conscience contemns. He is torn and tortured in an insoluble inner conflict.

[1] See, for instance, Wulf Sachs: Black Hamlet, 1937.

CHAPTER IV

TRAGEDY AND THE MIND OF THE INFANT

I AM AWARE that those Shakespearean critics who have enjoyed no special opportunities for penetrating into the obscurer aspects of mental activities, and who base their views of human motive on the surface valuation given by the agents themselves—to whom all conduct whether good or bad at all events springs from purely conscious sources—are likely to regard the suggestion put forward above as merely constituting one more of the extravagant and fanciful hypotheses of which the Hamlet literature in particular is so replete.[1] For the sake, however, of those who may be interested to apprehend the point of view from which this strange hypothesis seems probable I feel constrained to interpolate a few considerations on two matters that are not at all commonly appreciated at their true importance—namely, a child's feelings of jealousy and his attitude towards death.

The whole subject of jealousy in children is so clouded over with prejudice that even well-known facts are either ignored or are not estimated at their true significance. Stanley Hall, for instance, in his encyclopaedic treatise, makes a number of very just remarks on the importance of the subject in adolescence, but implies that before the age of puberty this passion is of relatively little con-

[1] A recent American critic (J. E. Hankins: The Character of Hamlet, 1941, p. 1) stigmatizes it as "an obvious brainstorm".

sequence. It was reserved for the genetic studies of psycho-analytic research to demonstrate the lasting and profound influence that infantile jealousies may have upon later character reactions and upon the whole course of a person's life.[1]

The close relation between adult jealousy and the desire for the removal of the rival by the most effective means, that of death, and also the common process of suppression of such feelings, is clearly illustrated in a remark of Stanley Hall's[2] to the effect that "Many a noble and even great man has confessed that mingled with profound grief for the death and misfortune of their best friends, they were often appalled to find a vein of secret joy and satisfaction, as if their own sphere were larger or better". He has doubtless in mind such passages as the following from La Rochefoucauld: "Dans l'adversité de nos meilleurs amis, il y a quelque chose qui ne nous déplait pas". A similar thought is more openly expressed by Bernard Shaw[3] when he makes Don Juan, in the Hell Scene, remark: "You may remember that on earth—though of course we never confessed it—the death of any one we knew, even those we liked best, was always mingled with a certain satisfaction at being finally done with them". Such cynicism in the adult is exceeded to an incomparable extent by that of the child, with its notorious, and to the parents often heartbreaking, egotism, with its undeveloped social instincts, and with its ignorance of the dread significance of death. A child very often unreasoningly interprets the various encroachments on its privileges, and the obstacles

---

[1] See, for instance, J. C. Flügel's valuable work on The Psycho-Analytic Study of the Family (No. 3 of the Internat. Psycho-Analytical Library, 1921).

[2] Stanley Hall: Adolescence, 1908, Vol. I, p. 358.

[3] Bernard Shaw: Man and Superman, 1903, p. 94.

interposed to the immediate gratification of its desires, as meaningless cruelty, and the more imperative is the desire that has been thwarted the more pronounced is the hostility towards the agent of this supposed cruelty, most often of course a parent. The most important encroachment, and the most frequent, is that made on the child's desire for affection. The resulting hostility is very often seen on the occasion of the birth of a subsequent child, and is usually regarded with amusement as an added contribution to the general gaiety called forth by the happy event. When a child, on being told that the doctor has brought him another playfellow, responds with the cry "Tell him to take it away again", he intends this, however, not, as is commonly believed, as a joke for the entertainment of his elders, but as an earnest expression of his intuition that in future, unless his *cri de coeur* be complied with, he will have to renounce his previously unquestioned pre-eminence in the family circle, a matter that to him is serious enough.

The second point, on which there is also much misunderstanding, is that of the child's attitude towards the subject of death, it being commonly assumed that this is necessarily the same as that of an adult. When a child first hears of anyone's death, the only part of its meaning that he realizes is that the person is *no longer there*, a consummation which time and again he has fervently desired when being interfered with by the persons around him. It is only gradually that the grimmer implications of the phenomenon are borne in upon him. When, therefore, a child expresses the wish that a given person, even a near relative, would die, our feelings would not be so shocked as they sometimes are, were we to interpret the wish from the point of view of the child. The same remark applies to the dreams of adults in which the death of a near and dear relative takes place, dreams in which the underlying repressed wish is usually concealed by an emotion of grief. But on the other hand the significance of these death-wishes is not to be under-estimated, either, for the later conflicts they may give rise to can be of the utmost importance for the person's mental welfare, and this in spite of the fact that in the vast majority of cases they remain merely wishes. Not that they always remain wishes, even in children. Some years ago[1] I collected a series of murders committed by jealous young children, and, referring to the constant occurrence of jealousy between children in the same family, pointed out the possible dangers arising from the imperfect appreciation by children of the significance of death.

I have spoken of the child, but it is often overlooked that childhood (roughly speaking, between the ages of three and twelve) is preceded by another period, that of infancy, which is vastly more fateful for the future than anything that happens in childhood. The congeries of emotions, phantasies, and impulses, forgotten or never even conscious, that occupy the dawning mind was only made accessible to our knowledge when Freud devised his psycho-analytic method for penetrating to the unconscious mental layers. It has been made fuller by the direct application of that method to young children by Melanie Klein[2] and her fellow-workers. The main discoveries here may be summed up in the statement that, side by side with loving attitudes and peaceful contentment, there are always to be found mental processes reminiscent of the most primitive aspects of savage life of an intensity that is only faintly mirrored later on by

[1] In two editorial articles entitled "Infant Murderers" in the *British Journal of Children's Diseases*, Nov. 1904, p. 510, and June 1905, p. 270.

[2] Melanie Klein: The Psycho-Analysis of Children, 1932.

the distressing aspects of our international relations, including even the tortures and other atrocities. Violent and ruthless impulses of destruction (i.e. murder in adult language) follow on the inevitable minor privations of this period. The jealousies, hatreds, and murderous impulses of which signs may be detected in childhood are, in fact, the weakened derivatives of a very sinister inheritance we bring to the world and which somehow has to be worked through and chastened in the painful conflicts and emotions of infancy. To say that a later reaction to a situation is excessive is simply to say that contributions have been made to it by the unconscious, i.e. the still living infantile mind. Before humour and other aids to mental digestion make their appearance these aspects of the infant's mind are entirely tragic, and all the tragedies of poets are ultimately derived from them.

Of the infantile jealousies the most important, and the one with which we are here occupied, is that experienced by a boy towards his father. The precise form of early relationship between child and father is in general a matter of vast importance in both sexes and plays a predominating part in the future development of the child's character; the theme has been expounded in an interesting essay by Jung,[1] where he gives it its due importance, though to the one-sided exclusion of the mother's influence. The only aspect that at present concerns us is the resentment felt by a boy towards his father when the latter disturbs, as he necessarily must, his enjoyment of his mother's exclusive affection. This feeling is the deepest source of the world-old conflict between father and son, between the younger and the older generation,

[1] Jung: "Die Bedeutung des Vaters für das Schicksal des Einzelnen", *Jahrbuch für psychoanalytische und psychopathologische Forschungen*, 1909, Bd. I.

the favourite theme of so many poets and writers, the central *motif* of most mythologies and religions. The fundamental importance that this conflict, and the accompanying breaking away of the child from the authority of his parents, has both for the individual and for society is clearly stated in the following passage of Freud's:[1] "The detachment of the growing individual from the authority of the parents is one of the most necessary, but also one of the most painful, achievements of development. It is absolutely necessary for it to be carried out, and we may assume that every normal human being has to a certain extent managed to achieve it. Indeed, the progress of society depends in general on this opposition of the two generations."

It was Freud[2] who first demonstrated, when dealing with the subject of the earliest manifestations of the sexual instinct in children, that the conflict in question rests in the last resort on sexual grounds. He has shown[3] that this instinct does not, as is generally supposed, differ from other biological functions by suddenly leaping into being at the age of puberty in all its full and developed activity, but that like other functions it undergoes a gradual evolution and only slowly attains the particular form in which we know it in the adult. A child has to learn how to love just as it has to learn how to walk, although the former function is so much more intricate and delicate in its adjustment than the latter that the development of it is a correspondingly slower and more involved process.

---

[1] Personal communication quoted by Rank: Der Mythus von der Geburt des Helden, 1909, S. 64.

[2] Freud: Die Traumdeutung, 1900, S. 176–80. He has strikingly illustrated the subject in a detailed study of a young boy: "Analyse der Phobie eines fünfjährigen Knaben", *Jahrbuch für psychoanalytische und psychopathologische Forschungen*, 1909, Bd. I.

[3] Freud: Drei Abhandlungen zur Sexualtheorie, 4. Aufl. 1920.

The earliest sexual manifestations are so palpably unadapted to what is generally considered to be the ultimate aim of the function, and are so general and tentative in contrast with the relative precision of the later ones, that the sexual nature of them is commonly not recognized at all.

This important theme cannot be further pursued here, but it must be mentioned how inevitably these earliest dim awakenings are evoked by the intimate physical relations existing between the child and the persons of his immediate environment, above all, therefore, his mother. When the attraction exercised by the mother is excessive it may exert a controlling influence over the boy's later destiny; a mass of evidence in demonstration of this, too extensive to refer to in detail, has been published in the psycho-analytical literature. Of the various results that may be caused by the complicated interaction between this influence and others, only one or two need be mentioned. If the awakened passion undergoes an insufficient "repression", then the boy may remain throughout life abnormally attached to his mother and unable to love any other woman, a not uncommon cause of bachelorhood. He may be gradually weaned from the attachment if it is less strong, though it often happens that the weaning is incomplete so that he is able to fall in love only with women who in some way resemble the mother; the latter occurrence is a frequent cause of marriage between relatives, as has been interestingly pointed out by Abraham.[1] The maternal influence may also manifest itself by imparting a strikingly tender feminine side to the later character.[2] When, on the other hand, the

[1] Abraham: "Verwandtenehe und Neurose", *Neurologisches Zentralblatt*, 1908, S. 1150.

[2] This trait in Hamlet's character has often been the subject of comment. See especially Bodenstedt: "Hamlet", *Westermanns Illustrierte*

aroused feeling is intensely "repressed" and associated with shame, guilt, and similar reactions the submergence may be so complete as to render the person incapable of experiencing any feeling at all of attraction for the opposite sex; to him all women are as forbidden as his mother. This may declare itself in pronounced misogyny or even, when combined with other factors, in actual homosexuality, as Sadger[1] has shown.

The attitude towards the successful rival, namely the father, also varies with—among other factors—the extent to which the aroused feelings have been "repressed". If this is only slight, then the natural resentment against the father may be more or less openly manifested later on, a rebellion which occurs commonly enough, though the true meaning of it is not recognized. To this source many social revolutionaries—perhaps all—owe the original impetus of their rebelliousness against authority, as can often be plainly traced—for instance, with Shelley and Mirabeau.[2] The unimpeded train of thought in the unconscious logically culminates in the idea, or rather the wish, that the father (or his substitute) may disappear from the scene, i.e. that he may die. Shakespeare himself provides a good example of this (King Henry IV, Part II) in the scene between the dying King and his son:

Monatshefte, 1865; Vining's suggestion that Hamlet really was a woman has been mentioned earlier in the present essay. That the same trait was a prominent one of Shakespeare's himself is well known (see, for instance, Bradley's works), a fact which the appellation of "Gentle Will" sufficiently recalls; Harris (op. cit., p. 273) even writes: "Whenever we get under the skin, it is Shakespeare's femininity which startles us."

[1] Sadger: "Fragment der Psychoanalyse eines Homosexuellen", *Jahrbuch für sexuelle Zwischenstufen*, 1908, Bd. IX; "Ist die konträre Sexualempfindung heilbar?", *Zeitschrift für Sexualwissenschaft*, Dez. 1908; "Zur Aetiologie der konträren Sexualempfindung", *Medizinische Klinik*, 1909, Nr. 2.

[2] See Wittels: Tragische Motive, 1911, S. 153.

Prince Henry. I never thought to hear you speak again.
King Henry. Thy wish was father, Harry, to that thought.

If, on the other hand, the "repression" is considerable, then the hostility towards the father will be correspondingly concealed from consciousness; this is often accompanied by the development of the opposite sentiment, namely of an exaggerated regard and respect for him, and a morbid solicitude for his welfare, which completely cover the underlying relationship.

The complete expression of the "repressed" wish is not only that the father should die, but that the son should then espouse the mother. Diderot[1] with astonishing intuition openly expressed this painful idea. "If we were left to ourselves and if our bodily strength only came up to that of our phantasy we would wring our fathers' necks and sleep with our mothers."[2] The attitude of son to parents is so transpicuously illustrated in the Oedipus legend,[3] as developed for instance in Sophocles' tragedy, that the group of mental processes in question is generally known under the name of the "Oedipus-complex".

We are now in a position to expand and complete

[1] Le Neveu de Rameau.

[2] ("Si le petit sauvage était abandonné a lui-même, qu'il conserva toute son imbécillité et qu'il réunit un peu de raison de l'enfant au berceau la violence des passions de l'homme de trente ans, il torderait le cou à son père et coucherait avec sa mère.) But even Diderot could not know that the violence of an infant's passion transcends that of any man at thirty, however alarming the latter may be for other people.

[3] See Freud: Die Traumdeutung, 1900, S. 181. Valuable expositions of the mythological aspects of the subject are given by Abraham, Traum und Mythus, 1909, and Otto Rank, op. cit. Rank has also worked through in great detail the various ways in which the same theme is made use of in literature: Das Inzest-Motiv in Dichtung und Sage, 1912, especially Kap. VIII, which contains an excellent analysis of the Oedipus legend.

the suggestions offered above in connection with the Hamlet problem.[1] The story thus interpreted would run somewhat as follows.

As a child Hamlet had experienced the warmest affection for his mother, and this, as is always so, had contained elements of a disguised erotic quality, still more so in infancy. The presence of two traits in the Queen's character accord with this assumption, namely her markedly sensual nature and her passionate fondness for her son. The former is indicated in too many places in the play to need specific reference, and is generally recognized. The latter is also manifest: Claudius says, for instance (Act IV, Sc. 7), "The Queen his mother lives almost by his looks". Nevertheless Hamlet appears to have with more or less success weaned himself from her and to have fallen in love with Ophelia. The precise nature of his original feeling for Ophelia is a little obscure. We may assume that at least in part it was composed of a normal love for a prospective bride, though the extravagance of the language used (the passionate need for absolute certainty, etc.) suggests a somewhat morbid frame of mind. There are indications that even here the influence of the old attraction for the mother is still exerting itself. Although some writers,[2] following Goethe,[3] see in Ophelia many traits of resemb-

[1] Here, as throughout this essay, I closely follow Freud's interpretation given in the footnote previously referred to. He there points out the inadequacy of the earlier explanations, deals with Hamlet's feelings towards his mother, father, and uncle, and mentions two other matters that will presently be discussed, the significance of Hamlet's reaction against Ophelia and of the probability that the play was written immediately after the death of Shakespeare's own father.

[2] e.g. G. Brandes: William Shakespeare, 1898, Vol. II, p. 48, who remarks that Hamlet's talk to Ophelia could be translated as "You are like my mother; you could behave like her".

[3] Goethe: Wilhelm Meister, IV, 14. "Her whole being hovers

lance to the Queen, perhaps just as striking are the traits contrasting with those of the Queen. Whatever truth there may be in the many German conceptions of Ophelia as a sensual wanton[1]—misconceptions that have been questioned by Loening[2] and others—still the very fact that it needed what Goethe happily called the "innocence of insanity" to reveal the presence of any such libidinous thoughts demonstrates in itself the modesty and chasteness of her habitual demeanour. Her naïve piety, her obedient resignation, and her un-reflecting simplicity sharply contrast with the Queen's character, and seem to indicate that Hamlet by a charac-teristic reaction towards the opposite extreme had un-knowingly been impelled to choose a woman who should least remind him of his mother. A case might even be made out for the view that part of his courtship originated not so much in direct attraction for Ophelia as in an unconscious desire to play her off against his mother, just as a disappointed and piqued lover so often has resort to the arms of a more willing rival. It would not be easy otherwise to understand the readiness with which he later throws himself into this part. When, for instance, in the play scene he replies to his mother's request to sit by her with the words "No, good mother, here's metal more attractive" and proceeds to lie at Ophelia's feet, we seem to have a direct indication of this attitude; and his coarse familiarity and bandying of ambiguous jests with the woman he has recently so ruthlessly jilted are hardly

---

in ripe, sweet voluptuousness". "Her fancy is moved, her quiet modesty breathes loving desire, and should the gentle Goddess Opportunity shake the tree the fruit would at once fall".

[1] For instance, Storffrich: Psychologische Aufschlüsse über Shake-speares Hamlet, 1859, S. 131; Dietrich, op. cit., S. 129; Tieck, Dramaturgische Blätter, II, S. 85, etc.

[2] Loening: op. cit., Cap. XIII. "Charakter und Liebe Ophelias".

intelligible unless we bear in mind that they were carried out under the heedful gaze of the Queen. It is as if his unconscious were trying to convey to her the following thought: "You give yourself to other men whom you prefer to me. Let me assure you that I can dispense with your favours and even prefer those of a woman whom I no longer love." His extraordinary outburst of bawdiness on this occasion, so unexpected in a man of obviously fine feeling, points unequivocally to the sexual nature of the underlying turmoil.

Now comes the father's death and the mother's second marriage. The association of the idea of sexuality with his mother, buried since infancy, can no longer be concealed from his consciousness. As Bradley[1] well says: "Her son was forced to see in her action not only an astounding shallowness of feeling, but an eruption of coarse sensuality, 'rank and gross,' speeding post-haste to its horrible delight". Feelings which once, in the infancy of long ago, were pleasurable desires can now, because of his repressions, only fill him with repulsion. The long "repressed" desire to take his father's place in his mother's affection is stimulated to unconscious activity by the sight of someone usurping this place exactly as he himself had once longed to do. More, this someone was a member of the same family, so that the actual usurpation further resembled the imaginary one in being incestuous. Without his being in the least aware of it these ancient desires are ringing in his mind, are once more struggling to find conscious expression, and need such an expenditure of energy again to "repress" them that he is reduced to the deplorable mental state he himself so vividly depicts.

There follows the Ghost's announcement that the father's death was a willed one, was due to murder.

[1] Bradley: op. cit., p. 118.

Hamlet, having at the moment his mind filled with natural indignation at the news, answers normally enough with the cry (Act I, Sc. 5):

> Haste me to know 't, that I with wings as swift
> As meditation or the thoughts of love,
> May sweep to my revenge.

The momentous words follow revealing who was the guilty person, namely a relative who had committed the deed at the bidding of lust.[1] Hamlet's second guilty wish had thus also been realized by his uncle, namely to procure the fulfilment of the first—the possession of the mother—by a personal deed, in fact by murder of the father. The two recent events, the father's death and the mother's second marriage, seemed to the world to have no inner causal relation to each other, but they represented ideas which in Hamlet's unconscious fantasy had always been closely associated. These ideas now in a moment forced their way to conscious recognition in spite of all "repressing forces", and found immediate expression in his almost reflex cry: "O my prophetic soul! My uncle?". The frightful truth his unconscious had already intuitively divined, his consciousness had now to assimilate as best it could. For the rest of the interview Hamlet is stunned by the effect of the internal conflict thus re-awakened, which from now on never ceases, and into the essential nature of which he never penetrates.

One of the first manifestations of the awakening of the old conflict in Hamlet's mind is his reaction against Ophelia. This is doubly conditioned by the two opposing

[1] It is not maintained that this was by any means Claudius' whole motive, but it was evidently a powerful one and the one that most impressed Hamlet.

attitudes in his own mind. In the first place, there is a complex reaction in regard to his mother. As was explained above, the being forced to connect the thought of his mother with sensuality leads to an intense sexual revulsion, one that is only temporarily broken down by the coarse outburst discussed above. Combined with this is a fierce jealousy, unconscious because of its forbidden origin, at the sight of her giving herself to another man, a man whom he had no reason whatever either to love or to respect. Consciously this is allowed to express itself, for instance after the prayer scene, only in the form of extreme resentment and bitter reproaches against her. His resentment against women is still further inflamed by the hypocritical prudishness with which Ophelia follows her father and brother in seeing evil in his natural affection, an attitude which poisons his love in exactly the same way that the love of his childhood, like that of all children, must have been poisoned. He can forgive a woman neither her rejection of his sexual advances nor, still less, her alliance with another man. Most intolerable of all to him, as Bradley well remarks, is the sight of sensuality in a quarter from which he had trained himself ever since infancy rigorously to exclude it. The total reaction culminates in the bitter misogyny of his outburst against Ophelia, who is devastated at having to bear a reaction so wholly out of proportion to her own offence and has no idea that in reviling her Hamlet is really expressing his bitter resentment against his mother.[1] "I have heard of your paintings too, well

[1] His similar tone and advice to the two women show plainly how closely they are identified in his mind. Cp. "Get thee to a nunnery: why wouldst thou be a breeder of sinners?" (Act III, Sc. 2) with "Refrain to-night; And that shall lend a kind of easiness To the next abstinence" (Act III, Sc. 4).
The identification is further demonstrated in the course of the

enough; God has given you one face, and you make
yourselves another; you jig, you amble, and you lisp,
and nickname God's creatures, and make your wanton-
ness your ignorance. Go to, I'll no more on 't; it hath
made me mad" (Act III, Sc. 1). On only one occasion
does he for a moment escape from the sordid implication
with which his love has been impregnated and achieve
a healthier attitude towards Ophelia, namely at the open
grave when in remorse he breaks out at Laertes for
presuming to pretend that his feeling for her could
ever equal that of her lover. Even here, however, as
Dover Wilson[1] has suggested, the remorse behind his
exaggerated behaviour springs not so much from grief at
Ophelia's death as from his distress at his bad conscience
that had killed his love—he acts the lover he fain would
have been.

Hamlet's attitude towards Ophelia is still more complex. Dover Wilson[2] has adduced good evidence for
thinking that Hamlet is supposed to have overheard the
intrigue in which Polonius "looses" his daughter to test
her erstwhile lover, a suggestion which had previously
been made by Quincy Adams[3]. This is probably an echo
of the old (Saxo) saga in which the girl is employed by
the king to test his capacity for sexual love and so
decide whether he is an imbecile or a cunning enemy.
It certainly helps to explain the violence with which he
attacks her feminine charms and treats her worse than a
paid prostitute. He feels she is sent to lure him on and
then, like his mother, to betray him at the behest of

play by Hamlet's killing the men who stand between him and these
women (Claudius and Polonius).

[1] op. cit., p. 270.

[2] op. cit., p. 128, etc.

[3] J. Q. Adams: "Commentary" in his edition of "Hamlet, Prince
of Denmark", 1929, p. 255.

another man. The words "Get thee to a nunnery"[1] thus
have a more sinister connotation, for in Elizabethan, and
indeed in later, times this was also a term for a brothel;
the name "Covent Garden" will elucidate the point to
any student of the history of London.

The underlying theme relates ultimately to the splitting
of the mother image which the infantile unconscious
effects into two opposite pictures: one of a virginal
Madonna, an inaccessible saint towards whom all
sensual approaches are unthinkable, and the other of a
sensual creature accessible to everyone. Indications of
this dichotomy between love and lust (Titian's Sacred
and Profane Love) are to be found later in most men's
sexual experiences. When sexual repression is highly
pronounced, as with Hamlet, then both types of women
are felt to be hostile: the pure one out of resentment at
her repulses, the sensual one out of the temptation she
offers to plunge into guiltiness. Misogyny, as in the play,
is the inevitable result.

The intensity of Hamlet's repulsion against woman in
general, and Ophelia in particular, is a measure of the
powerful "repression" to which his sexual feelings are
being subjected. The outlet for those feelings in the
direction of his mother has always been firmly dammed,
and now that the narrower channel in Ophelia's direction
has also been closed the increase in the original direction
consequent on the awakening of early memories tasks
all his energy to maintain the "repression". His pent-up
feelings find a partial vent in other directions. The
petulant irascibility and explosive outbursts called
forth by his vexation at the hands of Guildenstern and

[1] This exhortation (with its usual connotation of chastity) may
be equated with the one addressed later to his mother, "Go not
to my uncle's bed", indicating Hamlet's identification of the two
women in his feelings.

Rosencrantz, and especially of Polonius, are evidently to be interpreted in this way, as also is in part the burning nature of his reproaches to his mother. Indeed, towards the end of his interview with his mother the thought of her misconduct expresses itself in that almost physical disgust which is so characteristic a manifestation of intensely "repressed" sexual feeling.

> Let the bloat king tempt you again to bed,
> Pinch wanton on your cheek, call you his mouse,
> And let him for a pair of reechy kisses,
> Or paddling in your neck with his damn'd fingers,
> Make you to ravel all this matter out (Act III, Sc. 4)

Hamlet's attitude towards Polonius is highly instructive. Here the absence of family tie and of other similar influences enables him to indulge to a relatively unrestrained extent his hostility towards what he regards as a prating and sententious dotard.[1] The analogy he effects between Polonius and Jephthah[2] is in this connection especially pointed. It is here that we see his fundamental attitude towards moralizing elders who use their power to thwart the happiness of the young, and not in the over-drawn and melodramatic portrait in which he delineates his father: "A combination and a form indeed, where every god did seem to set his seal to give the world assurance of a man".

[1] It is noteworthy how many producers and actors seem to accept Hamlet's distorted estimate of Polonius, his garrulity being presumably an excuse for overlooking the shrewdness and soundness of his worldly wisdom. After all, his diagnosis of Hamlet's madness as being due to unrequited love for Ophelia was not so far from the mark, and he certainly recognized that his distressful condition was of sexual origin.

[2] What Shakespeare thought of Jephthah's behaviour towards his daughter may be gathered from a reference in Henry VI, Part III, Act V, Sc. 1. See also on this subject Wordsworth: On Shakespeare's Knowledge and Use of the Bible, 1864, p. 67.

It will be seen from the foregoing that Hamlet's attitude towards his uncle-father is far more complex than is generally supposed. He of course detests him, but it is the jealous detestation of one evil-doer towards his successful fellow. Much as he hates him, he can never denounce him with the ardent indignation that boils straight from his blood when he reproaches his mother, for the more vigorously he denounces his uncle the more powerfully does he stimulate to activity his own unconscious and "repressed" complexes. He is therefore in a dilemma between on the one hand allowing his natural detestation of his uncle to have free play, a consummation which would stir still further his own horrible wishes, and on the other hand ignoring the imperative call for the vengeance that his obvious duty demands. His own "evil" prevents him from completely denouncing his uncle's, and in continuing to "repress" the former he must strive to ignore, to condone, and if possible even to forget the latter; *his moral fate is bound up with his uncle's for good or ill.* In reality his uncle incorporates the deepest and most buried part of his own personality, so that he cannot kill him without also killing himself. This solution, one closely akin to what Freud[1] has shown to be the motive of suicide in melancholia, is actually the one that Hamlet finally adopts. The course of alternate action and inaction that he embarks on, and the provocations he gives to his suspicious uncle, can lead to no other end than to his own ruin and, incidentally, to that of his uncle. Only when he has made the final sacrifice and brought himself to the door of death is he free to fulfil his duty, to avenge his father, and to slay his other self—his uncle.

[1] Freud: "Trauer und Melancholie", Vierte Sammlung kleiner Schriften, 1918, Kap. XX.

There are two moments in the play when he is nearest to murder, and it is noteworthy that in both the impulse has been dissociated from the unbearable idea of incest. The second is of course when he actually kills the King, when the Queen is already dead and lost to him for ever, so that his conscience is free of an ulterior motive for the murder. The first is more interesting. It is clear that Hamlet is a creature of highly charged imagination; Vischer[1], for instance, quite rightly termed him a "Phantasiemensch". As is known, the danger then is that phantasy may on occasion replace reality. Now Otto Rank[2], who uses the same term, has plausibly suggested that the emotionally charged play scene, where a nephew kills his uncle(!), and when there is no talk of adultery or incest, is in Hamlet's imagination an equivalent for fulfilling his task.[3] It is easier to kill the King when there is no ulterior motive behind it, no talk of mother or incest. When the play is over he is carried away in exultation as if he had really killed the King himself, whereas all he has actually done is to warn him and so impel him to sign a death warrant. That his pretext for arranging the play—to satisfy himself about Claudius' guilt and the Ghost's honesty—is specious is plain from the fact that *before* it he had been convinced of both and was reproaching himself for his neglect. When he then comes on

---

[1] F. T. Vischer: "Hamlet, Prinz von Dänemark", in Shakespeare Vorträge. Bd. I, 1899.

[2] Otto Rank: "Das Schauspiel in Hamlet", *Imago*, Jahrg. IV, S. 45.

[3] There is a delicate point here which may appeal only to psychoanalysts. It is known that the occurrence of a dream within a dream (when one dreams that one is dreaming) is always found when analysed to refer to a theme which the person wishes were "only a dream", i.e. not true. I would suggest that a similar meaning attaches to a "play within a play", as in "Hamlet". So Hamlet (as nephew) can kill the King in his imagination since it is "only a play" or "only in play".

the King praying, and so to speak finds him surprisingly still alive, he realizes that his task is still in front of him, but can only say "Now *might* I do it" (not "will"). He then expresses openly the unconscious thoughts of his infancy—the wish to kill the man who is lying with his mother ("in th' incestuous pleasure of his bed")—but he knows only too well that his own guilty motive for doing so would always prevent him. So there is no way out of the dilemma, and he blunders on to destruction.

The call of duty to kill his stepfather cannot be obeyed because it links itself with the unconscious call of his nature to kill his mother's husband, whether this is the first or the second; the absolute "repression" of the former impulse involves the inner prohibition of the latter also. It is no chance that Hamlet says of himself that he is prompted to his revenge "by heaven and hell".

In this discussion of the motives that move or restrain Hamlet we have purposely depreciated the subsidiary ones—such as his exclusion from the throne where Claudius has blocked the normal solution of the Oedipus complex (to succeed the father in due course)—which also play a part, so as to bring out in greater relief the deeper and effective ones that are of preponderating importance. These, as we have seen, spring from sources of which he is quite unaware, and we might summarize the internal conflict of which he is the victim as consisting in a struggle of the "repressed" mental processes to become conscious. The call of duty, which automatically arouses to activity these unconscious processes, conflicts with the necessity of "repressing" them still more strongly; for the more urgent is the need for external action the greater is the effort demanded of the "repressing" forces. It is his moral duty, to which his father exhorts him, to put an end to the incestuous activities of his mother (by killing Claudius), but his unconscious does not want to put an end to them (he being identified with Claudius in the situation), and so he cannot. His lashings of self-reproach and remorse are ultimately because of this very failure, i.e. the refusal of his guilty wishes to undo the sin. By refusing to abandon his own incestuous wishes he perpetuates the sin and so must endure the stings of torturing conscience. And yet killing his mother's husband would be equivalent to committing the original sin himself, which would if anything be even more guilty. So of the two impossible alternatives he adopts the passive solution of letting the incest continue vicariously, but at the same time provoking destruction at the King's hand. Was ever a tragic figure so torn and tortured!

Action is paralysed at its very inception, and there is thus produced the picture of apparently causeless inhibition which is so inexplicable both to Hamlet[1] and to readers of the play. This paralysis arises, however, not from physical or moral cowardice, but from that intellectual cowardice, that reluctance to dare the exploration of his inmost soul, which Hamlet shares with the rest of the human race. "Thus conscience does make cowards of us all."

[1] The situation is perfectly depicted by Hamlet in his cry (Act IV, Sc. 4):

> I do not know
> Why yet I live to say "this thing's to do",
> Sith I have cause, and will, and strength, and means,
> To do't.

With greater insight he could have replaced the word "will" by "pious wish", which, as Loening (op. cit., S. 246) points out, it obviously means. Oddly enough, Rolfe (op. cit., p. 23) quotes this very passage in support of Werder's hypothesis that Hamlet was inhibited by the thought of the external difficulties of the situation, which shows to what straits the supporters of this untenable hypothesis are driven.

CHAPTER V

THE THEME OF MATRICIDE

WHEN A MAN who has been betrayed is emotionally moved to murder, whom should he kill, the rival lover or the lady? It is a nice question. Some men answer it, in words or in deeds, one way, other men the other (Othello!), and in doing so reveal much of their deepest attitude towards the two sexes. By this is not necessarily meant that the sex whose member they kill is the one most hated, despite the obvious hostility of the act. There are other motives for murder besides pure hostility, and they are even more frequent. Often the person who is killed is the one whose behaviour arouses the more unendurable conflict within, and that may or may not be the more hated of the two.

One supposes that in primaeval ages, when the sexual instinct was more purely lustful and not often accompanied with tender love, the outraged man would always have made the former decision, would have slain the intruder and then probably castigated his property for her disobedience. When, however, as with civilized men, that instinct had become impregnated with a sense of guilt (originating in the conflict over incest), such solutions are not always so simple. Woman's sensuality may then, as countless poets have told us, be felt not merely as a source of attraction but as a snare leading to sin, destruction, and eternal damnation. This is probably the reason why female chastity has in most societies been insisted on, often cruelly enough. Men use it as a protection against unbridled desires, even if at a later stage it may itself turn into a further stimulus to desire.

The importance of female fidelity begins, as all things do, in infancy. In spite of the natural jealousy of which we have spoken earlier, there is no doubt that the mother's fidelity to her husband, and particularly their marital happiness together, helps the infant to build up defences against his sensual impulses and gradually to transform and divert them along more hopeful paths. Hence the frequently unfortunate results of divorces on the offspring of the broken marriage. Some children are by nature more dependent on this external aid for acquiring self-control than are others, and when this dependence is very pronounced the boy, or later on the man, is especially sensitive to the question of woman's chastity or sensuality and in extreme cases may be said to be at her mercy. In the erotomanic form of paranoia, for example, the patient is unable to feel love for a woman until *after* she has shown—real or imagined—signs of regard for him. The degree of this dependence is usually to be correlated with the amount of femininity in the man's constitution.

If the mother is unfaithful to her husband or unduly lascivious, particularly if she is unduly sensual with the boy himself (thus committing a symbolic incest), not only is a strain placed on the latter's efforts to develop more socially, but he is apt to protect himself by generating an aversion, a sense of disgust, or even actual hostility to the mother. Her behaviour has stirred things in him that he cannot endure and which may make his life or his sanity impossible. Were she to proceed even further, and commit incest itself, then she has broken down the barrier so valuable to the boy in coping with his own impulses. All things are then open to him in the classical Oedipus direction, killing his father and eloping with the mother, and the fears and guilt thus aroused may be beyond his powers of endurance. There is only one hope left—to put an end at all costs to her behaviour and even allow his resentment at the torment she has caused him to proceed to its logical outcome of destroying her life. This is probably the explanation of the unnatural deeds of matricide that from time to time occur.

Now Hamlet seems to be in some such situation as has just been depicted. Of the "carnal, bloody and unnatural acts" (i.e. adultery, murder, and incest) of which Horatio speaks at the end of the tragedy, Hamlet knew when the play opens only of the last one, the other two being imparted to him later by the Ghost. Yet at the outset, as Dover Wilson[1] remarks, "The hideous thought of incest is the monster present in Hamlet's mind throughout the First Soliloquy. It is that, far more than the indecent haste of the wedding, which makes 'all the uses of this world' seem 'weary, stale, flat and unprofitable', sullies his very flesh, causes him to long for death and prompts the bitter cry 'Frailty, thy name is woman'." Again he writes:[2] "Hamlet felt himself involved in his mother's lust; he was conscious of sharing her nature in all its weakness and grossness; the stock from which he sprang was rotten". Nothing could be more outspoken; nevertheless the author seems somehow to evade the obvious conclusion that Hamlet himself (not only his mother) harboured incestuous wishes. He drily remarks,[3] it is true, "This incest business is so important that it is scarcely possible to make too much of it", but apparently he still refers to Hamlet's sensitiveness to someone *else's* incestuous proclivities, not to his own—and it is the latter

---

[1] Dover Wilson: op. cit., p. 307.
[2] Idem: op. cit., p. 42.   [3] Idem: op. cit., p. 43.

that is the ultimate source of Hamlet's intolerable distress.

Even after the Ghost informs him of the adultery and murder, both of which he had evidently suspected, it is still his mother's incest that dominates his emotions. Waldock,[1] indeed, would regard Hamlet's hesitancy as throughout secondary to his preoccupation with the horror at it. As Dover Wilson[2] puts it: "It is the 'couch for luxury and damned incest' far more than the murder that transforms his imagination into 'as foul as Vulcan's stithy' ", and Furnivall[3] before him took the same view. Both the King and Queen have sinned against his beloved father, but without doubt Hamlet was more horrified at his mother's sinning even than at his uncle's.

It is not surprising, therefore, that some critics, e.g. Mauerhof,[4] Wulffen,[5] and others, have wondered whether Hamlet did not feel the need to save his mother from her sin as more important than avenging his father's murder. Henderson gives[6] the theme a romantic form by contending that Shakespeare used as his model for his hero the ideal courtier as portrayed by Castiglione, and that Hamlet's knightly sense of honour made him regard the salvation of his mother as more important than the killing of the King. The most obvious way of putting an end to the incest, and at the same time avenging his father, was of course to kill Claudius, but, as we saw in the previous chapter, there were paralysing reasons that made this impossible. Even if these could be overcome what would be the Queen's situation?

[1] A. J. A. Waldock: Hamlet, 1931, pp. 78, 95.
[2] Dover Wilson: op. cit., p. 306.   [3] Furnivall: op. cit., p. 37.
[4] E. Mauerhof: Über Hamlet, 1882, S. 19.
[5] Erich Wulffen: Shakespeare's Hamlet, ein Sexualproblem, 1913.
[6] W. B. D. Henderson: "Hamlet as a Castiglionean Courtier",
The McGill News, June, 1934.

Dover Wilson[1] considers that she would inevitably be disgraced, a proposition which is in itself very questionable, and that Hamlet could not face such an eventuality. The same objection holds here as with so many explanations: why ever did not Hamlet debate this difficulty in his soliloquies, and why did he keep repeating that he had no idea of what it was that hindered him from proceeding with his task?

There would seem to be this much truth in all those suggestions: that Hamlet's conception of his task differed somewhat from his father's. The latter was clear about the avenging of the murder (i.e. by killing Claudius), but was emphatic about sparing his wife and not punishing or in any way injuring her. Hamlet, on the other hand, was more concerned about putting an end to the incestuous relationship than about avenging the murder, though he never doubted it was his duty to do so. His difficulty was what to do about his mother, and he was by no means so inclined as his father to let her off lightly; in fact, he keeps reminding himself to be careful not to injure her, as if that was a dangerous propensity he had to keep in check. Dover Wilson[2] has even suggested that the Ghost's reappearance in the bedroom scene is for the purpose of urging him to confine his attentions to his uncle and to spare his mother.

There remained only the horrible idea of destroying his mother. Gelber[3] seems to hint at this when he speaks of Hamlet's choice being between the ruin of his mother or the ruin of himself, but it was an American psychiatrist, Frederic Wertham,[4] who first ventured to propound

[1] Dover Wilson: op. cit., pp. 98, 172, etc.
[2] idem: op. cit., pp. 172, 252.
[3] A. Gelber: Shakespeare'sche Probleme, 1891, p. 189.
[4] Frederic Wertham: "The Matricidal Impulse", *Journal of Criminal Psychopathology*, April 1944, p. 455.

the idea in its naked form. He has made a study of matricide, and has published a book[1] describing the investigation of an actual case where the sight of his mother's lechery and betrayal of his greatly loved father led a youth to this desperate expedient. Wertham gives the name of Orestes complex to indicate a son's impulse to kill his mother. Interestingly enough, it is by no means the only occasion in which the story of Orestes has been brought into connection with that of Hamlet. Sixty years ago a French writer[2] compared the two and concluded that "the story of Hamlet is in reality only that of Orestes under another name and in another land". Gilbert Murray[3] devoted a detailed study to the comparison between the two. In spite of the many similarities, however, notably what Murray delicately calls the "shyness about the mother-murder" and the "shadow of madness" that affects the two heroes, he cannot find any historical connection between the two legends, so presumably they owe their resemblance to a common appeal to something in human nature. He writes: "In plays like 'Hamlet' or the 'Agamemnon' or the 'Electra' we have certainly fine and flexible character study, a varied and well-wrought story, a full command of the technical instruments of the poet and the dramatist, but we have also, I suspect, an undercurrent of desires and fears and passions, long slumbering yet eternally familiar, which have for thousands of years lain near the root of our most intimate emotions and have

[1] idem: Dark Legend, 1947. See also H. A. Bunker: "Mother-Murder in Myth and Legend", *The Psycho-analytic Quarterly*, 1948, Vol. XVII, p. 470.

[2] Ernest Dugit: "Orest et Hamlet", *Annales de l'enseignement supérieur de Grenoble*, 1889, p. 143.

[3] Gilbert Murray: "Hamlet and Orestes", Annual Shakespeare Lecture of the British Academy, 1914 (reprinted in his Classical Tradition in Poetry, 1930).

been wrought into the fabric of our most magical dreams". This insight, however, deserts him when he concludes that both of the stories are ultimately based on "that prehistoric and world-wide ritual battle of Summer and Winter, of Life and Death". Florence Anderson[1] also discusses the same comparison, and asserts, "I am sure that Shakespeare knew much about Orestes when he recast the rude Amleth as the subtle, melancholy Hamlet". She differs from Gilbert Murray in thinking that there must have been a very old relationship between the two traditions.

With Hamlet, Wertham advanced the idea in a one-sided fashion as the sole explanation of Hamlet's dilemma. Actually matricidal impulses, which are familiar to psycho-pathologists, always prove to emanate from the Oedipus complex of which they are one facet, or—to change the metaphor—for which they are an attempted solution. The topic is akin to the question with which this chapter opened; does an outraged man slay the woman or the rival?

Let us now return to the play in the light of these considerations. The crucial situation is evidently the bedroom scene.[2] Before this, however, in the bitter talk with Ophelia, Hamlet says: "I could accuse me of such things that it were better my mother had not borne me". What does this dark saying portend? It sounds more sinister even than killing a king. And there is a slight difference between "had I never been borne" and "had

---

[1] F. M. B. Anderson: "The Insanity of the Hero—an Intrinsic Detail of the Orestes Vendetta", *Transactions of the American Philological Association*, 1927, p. 431.

[2] It is appropriate here to recall that in both the Danish Saxo story and the Icelandic Ambales version it is told of Hamlet that he used to *sleep* in his mother's chamber(!) (I. Gollancz: op. cit., pp. 88, 119).

my mother not borne me". Need the mother be mentioned, and for whom would it have been better? This
faint hint could not claim attention in itself, but much
more follows. Even in the same scene he tells Ophelia
that "those that are married already, all but one shall
live". It is generally assumed that the "one" is Claudius,
but at the moment his thoughts are only about women,
at whom he is railing. To the King and Queen the idea in
question is not foreign. Claudius warns his wife, "His
liberty is full of threats to all, To you yourself", and in
the bedroom scene the Queen exclaims in alarm, "What
wilt thou do? Thou wilt not murder me?" The curious
slip of the tongue, deliberate or otherwise, in which he
addresses Claudius as "dear mother" shows how similar
are his feelings about the two. He even explains this:

> Father and Mother is man and wife,
> Man and Wife is one flesh, and so my mother.

In psycho-analysis this idea, common in infancy, is
known by the somewhat portentous title of the "combined parent concept". It dates from the phantasy of the
parents in coitus, i.e. as one flesh.

On his way to his mother's bedroom Hamlet (Act III,
Sc. 2, l. 394) speaks the savage words:

> Now could I drink hot blood,
> And do such bitter business as the day
> Would quake to look on: soft, now to my mother—
> O heart, lose not thy nature, let not ever
> The soul of Nero enter this firm bosom,
> Let me be cruel not unnatural.
> I will speak daggers to her, but use none.

In this connection Dover Wilson, as with the matter of
Hamlet's incestuous proclivities, approaches very close
to the dreadful thought, though in neither case does he

quite reach it. He writes[1]: "For whom is this itching dagger intended?" He is going to his mother. But surely he does not intend to murder her? He is no Nero. "These murderous impulses must be kept in leash." He is no Nero in action, certainly, but has he Nero's heart? Why the allusion at this critical point to Nero of all people, the man who is reputed to have slept with his mother and then murdered her (presumably for a similar reason, inability to bear the guilt her continued presence evoked)?

T. S. Eliot[2] writes: "The essential emotion of the play is the feeling of a son towards a guilty mother. . . . Hamlet is dominated by an emotion which is inexpressible, because it is in *excess* of the facts as they appear". As they appear, yes, but not as they actually exist in Hamlet's soul. His emotions are inexpressible not for that reason, but because there are thoughts and wishes that no one dares to express even to himself. We plumb here the darkest depths.

[1] op. cit., p. 244.   [2] loc. cit.

CHAPTER VI

THE HAMLET IN SHAKESPEARE

HAVING NOW braved the critics by investigating the unconscious mind of someone who never existed I may hope to have fortified rather than weakened the dramatist's aim in creating the illusion of Hamlet's being a living person. But this illusion had a validity behind it. It was a living person who imagined the figure of Hamlet with his behaviour, his reflections, and his emotions. The whole came from somewhere within Shakespeare's mind, and evidently from the inmost depths of that mind. Our search, therefore, must now continue in that direction, and this time there can be no question of any illusion. We return to the subject from which we started, namely poetic creation, and in this connection we have to inquire into the relation of Hamlet's conflict to the inner workings of Shakespeare's mind. It is here maintained that this conflict is an echo of a similar one in Shakespeare himself, as indeed it is to a greater or lesser extent with all men. There must be some correspondence, however disguised or transformed, between feelings a poet describes and feelings he has himself experienced in some form. The act of creation would otherwise be quite incomprehensible; *ex nihilo nihil fit.*

As was remarked earlier in this essay, the view that Shakespeare depicted in Hamlet the most important part of his own inner self is a widespread and doubtless a correct one.[1] Many of the passages in the soliloquies in particular, where Hamlet bares his soul—for example, the complaint about "th'oppressor's wrong, the proud man's contumely, the pangs of disprized love, the law's delay, the insolence of office, and the spurns that patient merit of th'unworthy takes"—are singularly inappropriate to the Danish prince and heir to the throne, while they are only too likely to have represented Shakespeare's personal experiences. Boas[2] writes: "Shakespeare makes the impression of choosing a theme as the vehicle of thoughts which were surging in his own breast. It may be confidently maintained that only out of an overwhelming subjective impulse could 'Hamlet' have arisen." He contends further: "The inference is irresistible that Shakespeare at some time must have felt himself in a peculiar degree susceptible to Hamlet's weakness"; we have to translate the word "weakness" by paralysis from the repression of incestuous and murderous impulses. Bradley,[3] who says that in Hamlet Shakespeare wrote down his own heart, makes the interesting comment: "We do not feel that the problems presented to most of the tragic heroes could have been fatal to Shakespeare himself. The immense breadth and clearness of his intellect would have saved him from the fate of Othello, Troilus, or Antony. We do feel, I think, and he himself may have felt, that he could not have coped with Hamlet's problem". In accord with this, but far profounder than the simple identification of Shakespeare with Hamlet, is Ella Sharpe's penetrating

[1] See especially Döring: Shakespeare's Hamlet seinem Grundgedanken und Inhalte nach erläutert, 1865; Taine: Histoire de la littérature anglaise, 1866, t. II, p. 254; Vischer: Altes und Neues, 1882, Heft 3; Hermann: Ergänzungen und Berichtigungen der hergebrachten Shakespeare-Biographie, 1884.

[2] F. S. Boas: Shakespeare and his Predecessors, 1896, p. 388.

[3] Bradley: Oxford Lectures on Poetry, 1909, p. 357.

remark:[1] "The poet is not Hamlet. Hamlet is what he might have been if he had not written the play of 'Hamlet' ". Here we have the Aristotelian function of tragedy once more illustrated, as well for the poet as for his audience. Heine[2] also understood the inner connection between mental suffering (nowadays called "neurotic illness") and the need of relief through poetic creation.

> Krankheit ist wohl der letzte Grund
> Des ganzen Schöpfungdrangs gewesen;
> Erschaffend konnte ich genesen,
> Erschaffend wurde ich gesund.

> (It was through illness I discovered
> This urge, this my creative zeal.
> As I created I recovered,
> Creating I achieved my weal.)

Chapman[3] beautifully expresses a similar idea. "It is as if he had passed through the valley of the shadow of death, and had come out among the stars". T. S. Eliot[4] wonders "why Shakespeare attempted to tackle the problem at all is an insoluble puzzle; under what compulsion he attempted to express the inexpressible we cannot ever know".

How very different all this sounds from Keats's description of the early Shakespeare as "the only perfectly happy creature whom God ever formed". Through what heartrending experience had he passed since then from which he was to emerge enriched with the ability to

---

[1] Ella Sharpe: "The Impatience of Hamlet", *International Journal of Psycho-Analysis*, 1929, Vol. X, p. 272.

[2] Heine: Neue Gedichte, Schöpfunglieder, 7.

[3] J. A. Chapman: Papers on Shakespeare. I. Hamlet, 1932, p. 24.   [4] T. S. Eliot: The Sacred Wood, 1920, p. 94.

sound the deepest chords in his nature? There is good reason to think that a highly significant change in his personality took place when he was about thirty-six years old.[1] As Dover Wilson says,[2] "a strain of sex nausea runs through almost everything Shakespeare wrote after 1600", and to this we must add the important theme of jealousy. He now entered on his tragic period, for, with the exception of "Romeo and Juliet", which is on a quite different plane, all his tragedies were composed after that date.[3] "The turning point in Shakespeare's prevailing mood must be placed in or about the year 1601".[4] "Throughout the great tragic period of Shakespeare's work, one of the prevailing notes towards the whole sex-question is of absolute nausea and abhorrence."[5]

A great change in personality can ensue only on a deep emotional experience. Have we any chance of discovering this with a poet about whose personal life so little is known? T. S. Eliot is of course right when he says we can never know, but perhaps we can approach nearer and divine at least something of its nature. Everything points to the creation of Hamlet as being in some way an

[1] See Dover Wilson: op. cit., p. 306. He regards "Hamlet" as representing the "turning point in Shakespeare's spiritual and artistic development" (Introduction to his Edition of "Hamlet", p. viii).

[2] idem: The Essential Shakespeare, 1932, pp. 48–9.

[3] A. S. Cairncross (The Problem of Hamlet, 1936), it is true, has recently tried to prove that the tragedies were all written in Shakespeare's youth ("Hamlet" in particular dating from 1588!), but he has found no support for this startling view. The most his evidence and argument would seem to suggest is that Shakespeare had a hand, perhaps even ten or twelve years earlier, in writing the "Hamlet" that then Kyd took up, but the play "Hamlet", *as we know it*, must surely have been fundamentally rewritten after the turn of the century.

[4] G. Brandes: "Hamlet" in William Shakespeare, 1926, Vol. I, p. 313.   [5] D. Figgis: op. cit., p. 284.

expression of that great personal experience, or—put more cautiously—a way of responding to it. Apparently he wrote nothing for two years after it. We therefore inquire into anything known of Shakespeare's life at that particular juncture, but to do so we must first ascertain when that was.

The exact source of Shakespeare's plot and the date at which he wrote the play are two of the knottiest problems in the history of English literature, and we shall see that they both possess a considerable interest for our purpose. To know precisely what versions of the Hamlet story were accessible to Shakespeare before he wrote his play would tell us what were his own contributions to it, a piece of knowledge that would be invaluable for the study of his personality. Again, to know the exact date of his composition might enable us to connect the impulse to write the play with significant events in his own life.

As far as has been at present ascertained, the facts seem to be somewhat as follows. Shakespeare must certainly have taken not only the skeleton of the plot, but also a certain amount of detail,[1] from earlier writings. It is not absolutely known, however, which of these he had actually read, though it is probable that most of the following sources were available to him, all derived from the Hamlet legend as narrated early in the thirteenth century by Saxo Grammaticus in the third book of his *Historia Danica*. This was printed, in Latin, in 1514, translated into German by Hans Sachs in 1558, and into French by Belleforest about 1570.[2] It is very probable

[1] Though less than with most of his plays.
[2] Belleforest: Histoires tragiques (1564), t. V. 1570. This may have been derived directly from Saxo, but more likely from another intermediary now unknown.

that a rough English translation of Belleforest's version—
we say version rather than translation, for it contains
numerous modifications of the story as told by Saxo—
was extant throughout the last quarter of the sixteenth
century, but the only surviving copy, entitled "The
Hystorie of Hamblet", actually dates from 1608, and
Elze[1] has given reasons for thinking that whoever issued
it had first read an English "Hamlet", possibly Shakespeare's own. For at least a dozen years before Shakespeare wrote his "Hamlet" there was a drama of the
same name being played in England; references to it
were made in 1589 by Nash[2] and in 1596 by Lodge.[3]
The suggestion, first made by Malone[4] in 1821, that this
play is from the hand of Thomas Kyd has been strongly
confirmed by later research[5] and may now be regarded
as almost certainly established. There is contemporary
evidence[6] showing that it was played at the Newington
Butts theatre about 1594, then jointly occupied by the
Lord Chamberlain's company of which Shakespeare was
at that time a member. Henslowe incidentally makes it
plain that it was a very common practice for dramatists
to avail themselves freely of the material, whether of plot,
character, or even language, supplied by their predecessors or contemporaries, and, apart from the moral
certainty that Shakespeare must have been familiar
with this play and drawn on it for his own, there is good

[1] Elze: William Shakespeare, 1876.

[2] Nash: "To the Gentlemen Students of both Universities",
prefixed to Green's Menaphon, or Arcadia, 1589.

[3] Lodge: Wits miserie, and the Worlds madnesse, 1596.

[4] Malone: Variorum, 1821, Vol. II.

[5] See Widgery: op. cit., pp. 100 et seq.; Fleay: Chronicle of the
English Drama, 1891; Sarrazin: Thomas Kyd und sein Kreis, 1892:
Corbin: The Elizabethan Hamlet, 1895; Furnivall: Introduction
to the First Quarto in Shakespeare Quarto Facsimiles.

[6] Henslowe's Diary, 1609, reprinted by the Shakespeare Society,
1845.

reason for thinking that he incorporated actual parts of it in his "Hamlet".[1]

Now unfortunately no copy of Kyd's play has survived. We can compare Shakespeare's "Hamlet" with the Belleforest translation of Saxo's prose story and also with the English modification of this, the "Hystorie of Hamblet", both of which he *probably* used; but not with the Elizabethan play, which he almost *certainly* used. We therefore cannot tell with surety which of his deviations from the original story originated with Shakespeare and which of them were merely taken over from Kyd. And it is just from deviations such as these that we can learn much of the personality of the writer; they are unmistakably his own contributions, whether they consist in positive additions or in negative omissions.

Still the case is not quite so desperate as it seems. In the first place we have a copy—late, it is true, being printed only in 1710—of a German play, "Der bestrafte Brudermord oder Prinz Hamlet aus Dänemark", which was played at least as early as 1626 in Dresden, and which intrinsic evidence proves to emanate, at all events in great part, from a very early and probably pre-Shakespearean version of "Hamlet".[2] The differences between it and Shakespeare's "Hamlet" will be discussed later. In the second place a comparison can be instituted between "Hamlet" and the surviving plays of Kyd, for instance "The Spanish Tragedy", where there is also the theme of motiveless hesitation on the part of a hero who has to avenge his next-of-kin's murder. The characteristics of the two writers are so distinct that it is not

[1] See Sarrazin: op. cit.; and Robertson: The Problem of "Hamlet", 1919, pp. 34–41.

[2] Bernhardy: "Shakespeare's Hamlet. Ein literar-historisch kritischer Versuch," *Hamburger literarisch-kritische Blätter*, 1857; Shakespeare in Germany, 1865; Latham: Two Dissertations, 1872.

very difficult for expert critics to tell with which of them a given passage or part of a plot is likely to have originated. The third consideration is a purely psychological one. It is in the last resort not of such absorbing interest whether Shakespeare took only part of a plot or the whole of it from other sources; the essential point is that he took, or made, a plot of such a kind as to enable him to express his deepest personal feelings and thoughts. The intrinsic evidence from the play decisively shows that Shakespeare projected into it his inmost soul; the plot, whether he made it or found it, became his own, inasmuch as it obviously corresponded with the deepest part of his own nature. One has only for a moment to compare the treatment of the similar themes in "Hamlet" and in "The Spanish Tragedy" to realize how fundamentally different was Shakespeare's and Kyd's reaction to them.

In addition to these definite sources ruder accounts of the old Amleth[1] story, of Celtic and Norse origin, were widely spread in England, and the name Hamlet itself, or some modification of it, was common in the Stratford district.[2] Foreshadowing Ophelia, a certain Katherine Hamlet was drowned in the Avon a mile from Stratford in December 1579, when Shakespeare was fifteen years old; incidentally a relative of his, also called William Shakespeare, had been drowned in the same river six months before.[3] As is well known, Shakespeare in 1585 christened his only son Hamnet,[4] a frequent variant of the

[1] The name appears as Amhlaide in an Irish source of 919 and as Amlodi in an Icelandic one of 1230. Sir Israel Gollancz (The Sources of Hamlet, 1926, pp. 47, 54–6) gives reasons for thinking it had a Welsh origin. See also a correspondence on this in *Notes and Queries*, July to October, 1907.

[2] Elton: William Shakespeare. His Family and Friends, 1904, p. 223.   [3] See E. I. Fripp: Shakespeare Studies, 1930, p. 128.

[4] Hamlet and Hamnet were interchangeable names, even with

name; the boy died in 1596. For all these reasons it is plain that the plot of the tragedy must have been present in Shakespeare's mind for many years before it actually took form as a new composition. When exactly this happened is a matter of some uncertainty and considerable bearing.

"Hamlet" was actually registered at Stationers' Hall on July 26, 1602, with the words added "as it was lately acted". In 1603 appeared the notorious pirated edition in quarto (Q.1)[1], the official version (Q.2) following in 1604–5. In a recent remarkable textual study of the two quartos Dover Wilson[2] comes to the following conclusions. The first, pirated quarto and the second, definitely Shakespearean, one were derived from the same source, an actor's copy used in the theatre from 1593 onward. He dates Kyd's play as being before 1588 and thinks that Shakespeare partly revised this about 1591–2; this revision was mainly confined to the ghost scenes. The Elizabethan "Hamlet", therefore, used by the Lord Chamberlain Players in the sixteen-nineties would be a combination of Kyd's and Shakespeare's work, possibly recast by these and even by other dramatists from time to time. It is evident, however, that Shakespeare countered the 1602 piracy by issuing what was practically a rewritten play, and the dates go to confirm Freud's suggestion that this was done while he was still under the influence of the thoughts stirred by his father's death, an event which is usually the turning-point in the mental life of a man.

If Dover Wilson's conclusions prove to be correct, as

the same person (see A. Rhodes: "Hamlet as Baptismal Name in 1590", *Notes and Queries*, Nov. 4, 1911, p. 395).

[1] Discovered only in 1823!

[2] Dover Wilson: The Copy for "Hamlet", 1603, and the "Hamlet" Transcript, 1593; 1919.

seems probable, then we may have an answer to the riddle provided by Gabriel Harvey's marginal comments in his copy of Speght's Chaucer, which were presumably written before February 1601, as fixed by the date of Essex's death; in these he refers to Shakespeare's "Hamlet". Renewed interest in the point has been aroused by Moore Smith's[1] discovery of the copy in question which had been missing for over a century. The passage in Harvey and also the inferred dates are by no means unequivocal,[2] but even if the conclusion is accepted that it proves Shakespeare's "Hamlet" to have been in existence a couple of years before the date usually allotted to its composition there is left the possibility that the reference is to the early acting version only, which may well by that time have become more associated with Shakespeare's name than with Kyd's, and not to the play that we know as "Shakespeare's Hamlet".

Among the other details that have been relied on to date the play are the "innovation" (Act II, Sc. 2, l. 335) which is thought to refer to Essex's irrational attack on

[1] Moore Smith: Gabriel Harvey's Marginalia, 1913, pp. viii–xii, 225, and 232.

[2] For instance, the allusion to "our flourishing metricians" could well have included Essex even after his death in February 1601, since one of those he lists (the poet Watson) had died as long before as 1592; the reference to him (" The Earl of Essex commends Albion's England") was probably in the historic present. The date itself when Harvey made his note is doubtful, voices having been raised for 1598 (Boas: Shakespeare and the Universities, 1923, p. 27, 256, and most writers), 1600 (Lawrence: "The Date of Hamlet", Times Literary Supplement, April 8, 1926), or even 1605 (Gray: "The Date of Hamlet", Journal of English and Germanic Philology, 1932, Vol. XXXI, p. 51). Sir Edmund Chambers, who had dated "Hamlet" as being composed in 1600, later admitted that in doing so he had attached too much weight to Harvey's note and now revises the date to 1601 (E. K. Chambers: Shakespearean Gleanings, 1944, p. 68).

Queen Elizabeth, February 6, 1601, when, incidentally, the multitude proclaimed him in a way very reminiscent of Laertes' uprising in the play; the "inhibition" (Act II, Sc. 2, l. 336), referring either to the same event or else to the Privy Council Order of June 22, 1600, restricting the number of London theatres to two; the allusion in the "aery of children" (Act II Sc. 2, l. 342) to the "War of the Theatres"[1] which would give the summer of 1601 as the earliest date of the play;[2] and "we go to gain a little patch of ground that has in it no profit but the name" (Act IV, Sc. 4, l. 18), which has been thought to refer to the siege of Ostend that began late in June 1601. Sir Edmund Chambers[3] has protested about this last item that the official evidence, which he quotes in great detail, shows it as a place of considerable value, but it would seem that this is couched in military terms, while to the common man it might well appear uninviting enough—as many patches of Picardy fought over in the First World War did to our soldiers.[4]

A review of the various discussions yields the conclusion that most competent critics would agree with Dover Wilson[5] in attributing the date of "Hamlet" to the summer or autumn of 1601; some would give a slightly later date, certainly if the allusion to the siege of Ostend is substantiated. We therefore inquire into what is known of important events in Shakespeare's life

[1] See E. K. Chambers: The Elizabethan Stage, Vol. I, p. 381, Vol. III, p. 363.
[2] See C. W. Wallace: "The 'Hamlet' Passage on the Black-friar's Children", Ch. XIV of The Children of the Chapel of Blackfriars, 1908, p. 173. Wallace infers the date of the "Hamlet" composition as being late 1601 to early 1602.
[3] Op. cit., Gleanings, pp. 70 and 110.
[4] In a private communication Sir Edmund Chambers admits the justice of this criticism.
[5] Dover Wilson: Introduction to "Hamlet", p. xvii.

about or before this date. All we have are two facts and one surmise, and unfortunately it is the last of these that probably contains the secret we are searching for. The most certain fact is that the Earl of Essex was executed on February 25, 1601, i.e. before the writing of "Hamlet". In Essex's rising the Earl of Southampton, Shakespeare's earlier patron,[1] was involved, and, as we have occasion to know from modern "purges", the disastrous consequences of such incidents radiate far from the leaders to even remote subordinates or people distantly related to them. The Earl of Southampton, Shakespeare's patron, was still in prison awaiting an uncertain fate. Shakespeare and his company apparently managed to weather the storm, but it was probably an event of more than practical significance to him. Essex was a fascinating figure, the dominating one of his time, and Dover Wilson[2] has produced extensive evidence showing Shakespeare must have had him well in mind when depicting the impulsive, unstable, procrastinating,

---

[1] Nothing is known of Shakespeare's connection with him after 1594, though it may of course have continued.

[2] idem: The Essential Shakespeare, 1932, pp. 95–107. See also Hermann Conrad: "Robert Essex", *Shakespeare Jahrbuch*, 1881, Bd. XVI, S. 274 and 1895, Bd. LXXXI, S. 58, Fr. Lucy: "Eine Shakespeare-Studie (ist Essex das Urbild Hamlets? Nach Briefen von Essex an seine Schwester Lady Rich)", *Deutsches Montagsblatt*, Aug. 1, 1881, and Isaac: "Hamlet's Familie", *Shakespeare Jahrbuch*, Bd. XVI, S. 274.

William Herbert, later Earl of Pembroke, the alleged Mr. W. H. of the Sonnets, has also been claimed as a model for Hamlet (A. Döring: Hamlet, 1898, S. 35), though a better case can be made for his identification with Horatio (J. T. Foard: "The Genesis of Hamlet", *The Manchester Quarterly*, 1889, Vol. XV). Edward de Vere, seventeenth Earl of Oxford, whom post-Baconians have apparently adopted as their last hope, is also a candidate for the figure of Hamlet (Percy Allen: Shakespeare and Chapman as Topical Dramatists, 1929, Ch. IV). The identification with Sir Philip Sidney (Berawne: "Hamlet's Father", *The Stratford-on-Avon Herald*, Oct. 1, 1886) seems much more remote.

self-destroying character of Hamlet. Polonius, incidentally, is thought to be a caricature of Burleigh, the man
who foiled Essex, and Claudius of the Earl of Leicester,
who was believed to have murdered the previous
Earl of Essex after committing adultery with his wife (he
subsequently married the widow).

The other fact is that Shakespeare's father died in
September 1601. Unfortunately we have no data about
the cause of his death or how long he had been known
to be suffering from a fatal illness. Many years ago
Henderson[1] pointed out this conjuncture and argued
that it played an important part in the writing of "Hamlet"; he stresses the feeling of death throughout the
play, and notes that Shakespeare then turned from
comedy to tragedy. Rosner[2] considered that when
writing the play Shakespeare was in an "excessively
nervous condition" because of the death of his father and
the execution of Essex. Schücking[3] also observes the same
concatenation, and Freud[4] attached great significance
to it, remarking that to many men the death of the
father is perhaps the most important event in their life;
the moment when a man succeeds, i.e. replaces, his father
may revive the forbidden wishes of his infancy. The
dates and circumstances, however, are too indeterminate
to allow us to regard Freud's supposition from being any
more than an inspired guess, which, however, may be
greatly inspired. One might perhaps add in this connection that the only other play in which Shakespeare
depicted a son's intimate relation to his mother, "Corio-

[1] W. A. Henderson: "The Heart of Hamlet's Mystery", *Notes and Queries*, May 7, 1892, and Aug. 13, 1894.
[2] K. Rosner: Shakespeare's Hamlet im Lichte der Neuropatho-
logie, 1895.
[3] L. L. Schücking: Character Problems in Shakespeare's Plays,
1922, p. 162.   [4] loc. cit.

lanus" (cp. "the most noble mother of the world"),
was written just after the death of his mother in 1608
(though Frank Harris would doubtless retort that this
was also the year in which Mary Fitton finally left
London!).

We come last to the surmise. This may prove to be less
hypothetical than it sounds, even if we have to rely more
on internal than on external evidence; circumstantial
evidence is notoriously more often trustworthy than
direct evidence. It is surely plain that an emotional
experience to which Shakespeare responded by writing
"Hamlet" must correspond in its nature with the
underlying themes of the tragedy. Now it is true that
the two facts just mentioned, deaths of a father and of
an obvious father-substitute, accord in part with this
criterion, but we entirely miss in them any allusion to the
almost physical disgust at sex that is so prominent in
"Hamlet". Such a misogyny is hardly possible except
from a sense of bitter disappointment at the hands of the
opposite sex. This may be wholly constitutional, dating
from early childhood experiences, a state of affairs that
can be excluded when one thinks of the happy young
Shakespeare writing his love comedies, or only partly so
and then reinforced by a tremendous experience of the
same sort in adult life. What we would expect, therefore,
is some overwhelming passion that ended in a betrayal
in such circumstances that murderous impulses towards
the faithless couple were stirred but could not be admitted to consciousness.

Now, as is well known, Shakespeare himself in his
Sonnets gives an unmistakable description of just such
an experience, and from its intensity more critics than
not have regarded it as a personal one. It is a story of a
handsome young noble to whom Shakespeare is devoted

and (perhaps because of that) whom he foolishly introduced to his mistress of whom he was profoundly enamoured. The usual result followed. Within a year or two the young lady had an affair—we know not whether to call it a love affair or not—with the young noble, displacing the middle-aged poet. The poet depicts his sufferings, but it is notable that he rails against the lady far more than against his faithless friend, to whom indeed he soon becomes reconciled. It is evident that he had felt the loss of the friend more than that of the lady, whom he chiefly blames for what had happened.

A hundred and thirty years ago Heywood Bright, and a little later James Borden, independently, identified the Mr. W. H. to whom the Sonnets are dedicated with William Herbert, who became Earl of Pembroke in January 1601. Fifty years ago (Rev.) Harrison and Tylor[1] drew the natural inference that, this being so, we must also be able to identify the famous Dark Lady of the Sonnets with Mary Fitton.[2] Tylor investigated this clue very fully, and his conclusions have been amplified by some writers, e.g. Furnivall[3] himself. As reconstructed thus, the story runs as follows.

Mary Fitton became Maid of Honour to Queen Elizabeth in 1595 at the age of seventeen. There are indications that she had already been secretly married, and that her father later discovered it. There is no direct contemporary evidence that she ever knew Shake-

[1] T. Tylor: Shakespeare's Sonnets, 1890, and the Herbert-Fitton Theory, 1899. See also Georg Brandes: op. cit., Vol. I, Ch. VI. The subject is dealt with fully by these authors.

[2] Soon after Tylor's discovery came the disturbing news that a portrait of Mary Fitton in the possession of Lady Newdegate showed her to have had a *fair*, red-and-white complexion. Further investigation, however, made it more probable that it was a portrait of Miss Mildred Maxey.

[3] F. J. Furnivall: Shakespeare and Mary Fitton, 1897.

speare(!), although she is known to have been on rather familiar terms with a member of his company (Kemp). There is, however, some indirect evidence indicating that his passion for her dated from 1597. Many allusions to her apparently occur in "Love's Labour's Lost", which was presented at Court, when she was doubtless present, at Christmas of that year. It is to be presumed that the passion led to intimacy. Herbert came to London in the spring of 1598, and in 1600 she was meeting him surreptitiously. A child was born early in March 1601, when she was banished from Court, and Herbert sent to prison. Despite strong pressure he refused to marry her, and it has been suggested that was in part because of what Shakespeare told him of her character, since the breach between the two men did not last long. The Sonnets themselves have been dated as being written at various times between 1598 and 1601. Mary herself did not marry publicly until 1607 (a Captain Potwhele being this time the lucky man), but she produced two more bastards, this time by Sir Richard Leveson. She seems to have been, not a beautiful, but a very vivacious young person with some masculine traits. According to the Sonnets it was *she* who led young Herbert astray, and one would surmise that Shakespeare's devotion to her was of a slavish nature in which the feminine side of him also played its part. It is believed that he resumed his relations with her subsequently.

Frank Harris, who displays considerable insight here and there in spite of his erratic extravagances, has persuasively expounded the view that Shakespeare wrote "Hamlet" as a reaction to his deep disappointment at the double betrayal.

It is noteworthy that Shakespeare's famous victims of jealousy, Othello, Leontes, Posthumus, all display extraordinary credulousness, which at times makes the audience impatient with them, and have perfectly innocent wives. The crassest of them, Leontes, presents a pure case of delusional jealousy, and true to type actually begs Camillo to assure him that he has been cuckolded. This could mean that Shakespeare found the theme of a justified jealousy too painful for him to dwell on,[1] or else that he was so familiar with the unjustified kind as to be able to depict it to perfection. Both explanations may well be true. Extensive clinical experience of various types of jealousy[2] has shown that, far from being a response to an objective situation, jealousy is more often an attitude dictated from within by certain motives and, strange to say, often indicates a repressed wish for the betrayal. This state of affairs may so act on the partner as, so to speak, to drive her into infidelity, when the wished-for and dreaded climax is then reached. This is especially true of persons with a bisexual disposition, who therefore wish to play both a male and a female part in the triangular situation. On the basis of much experience in the study of such cases I venture to express the surmise that Shakespeare played an active part in bringing about the misfortune that then so deeply affected him. If it is true that he introduced Herbert to Mary Fitton two years before they betrayed him I can very well picture him as so boring her with praise of his beloved handsome youth that finally out of pique she took him at his word and "vamped" the boy. But

[1] In the extreme case of Leontes it is worthy of note that Shakespeare entirely suppressed the actual grounds for jealousy stated in Green's novel from which he took the plot.

[2] Freud: "Certain Neurotic Mechanisms in Jealousy, Paranoia and Homosexuality", (1922), Collected Papers, Vol. II; Ernest Jones: "La Jalousie", Address delivered at the Sorbonne, March 1929. (Reprinted as Ch. XVI of Papers on Psycho-Analysis, Fifth Edition, 1948.)

nothing is so terrible as the fulfilment of unacknowledged desires, and the reality of the betrayal must have been more crushing to Shakespeare than his previous teasing phantasies—the ones portrayed over and again in his dramas.

The following passages may be quoted[1]: Why did Hamlet hate his mother's lechery? Most men would hardly have condemned it, certainly would not have suffered their thoughts to dwell on it beyond the moment[2]; but to Hamlet his mother's faithlessness was horrible, shameful, degrading, simply(!) because Hamlet-Shakespeare had identified her with Miss Fitton, and it was Miss Fitton's faithlessness, it was her deception he was condemning in the bitterest words he could find. He thus gets into a somewhat unreal tragedy, a passionate intensity which is otherwise wholly inexplicable". According to Harris,[3] "The story of his idolatrous passion for Mary Fitton is "the story of his life" and he considers[4] that "Shakespeare owes the greater part of his renown to Mary Fitton".

The whole story sounds temptingly plausible and by no means out of accord with what we otherwise know of Shakespeare's personality. Alas, however, it appears also to exemplify the definition of a tragedy imputed to Herbert Spencer—"a beautiful theory slain by a nasty, ugly fact". For it all rests on one fatal assumption, that the dedication to the Sonnets was written with Shakespeare's knowledge and to express his attitude to a particular man. Now the sober Shakespeare critics, among the most knowledgeable of

[1] F. Harris: The Man Shakespeare, 1909, p. 269.
[2] In their judgement in this matter how much nearer Bradley (see p. 63) is than Harris to the fount of feeling.
[3] op. cit., p. 217.   [4] op. cit., p. 231.

whom is Sir Sidney Lee,[1] take an entirely different view of it. They maintain that Shakespeare had no hand in that publication, any more than he did with any of his plays, and that the "onlie begetter" to whom Thomas Thorpe who published the Sonnets dedicated them was not the inspirer of their poetry but merely a friendly mediocrity, by name William Hall, who was the "sole procurer" or owner of the manuscript. Herbert, although it is true his Christian name was William, was before his father's death always known by the courtesy title of Lord Herbert, and when Thorpe dedicated anything to him he did so in properly obsequious language; to have addressed him flippantly as "Mr W. H." would have been to provoke the sinister activity of the Star Chamber. So I am afraid we have to bow to the authorities, and to dismiss the Mary Fitton story as *ben trovato*. Nevertheless the Sonnets remain and cannot be so easily dismissed. They are assuredly written between 1593 and 1603, but when exactly is much disputed. Students of the literature of that period such as Sir Sidney Lee see no reason to find in them allusions to a personal experience; many others do. Whether Shakespeare "unlocked his heart" in them, or whether Browning was right in saying "If so, the less Shakespeare he", are matters that will long exercise our wits, nor may we even know who their Dark Lady was.

But for a psychologist it is hard to think that Shakespeare never passed through the experience they describe, which accords so well with the emotion he vividly portrays in all his great tragedies. Nor would he regard Shakespeare's attitude in it as that of a free man, i.e. one unburdened with unconscious "complexes". It is rather

[1] Sir Sidney Lee: *A Life of Shakespeare*, New Edition 1915, pp. 623, etc.

that of a bisexual man suffering from deep inner conflicts.
Harris may well be right in saying that behind Queen
Gertrude stands someone like Mary Fitton, but behind
that lady certainly stands Shakespeare's mother. Perhaps
the most notable feature in the story is that Shakespeare, in spite of anguished jealousy—and no one has
better described this emotion—was compelled by inner
motives to smother his natural resentment at the treatment he had received and was unable to express it
towards either the faithless friend or the faithless mistress;
it is an unnatural tolerance, surely an inhibition. His
way of responding was to compose a tragedy whose
theme was the suffering of a tortured man who could not
avenge his injured feelings (or even his parents' dishonour). In so doing he assuaged his own suffering and
saved his sanity of mind, though he could never be the
same happy man again and had still much to pass through
before he attained the repose of a premature death.

*   *

*

Although it is maintained here that the source of
Shakespeare's inspiration in the creation of Hamlet
lay in the deepest, i.e. the oldest, part of his being, one
which had been aroused once more by the catastrophic
experiences he had passed through soon before he
composed the tragedy (the theme of which had long
echoed through his mind), it is of course evident that
he was also influenced by many other current experiences. Never was there a play so replete with allusions,
only some of which have been since interpreted. We have
even something of the men he had in mind, besides
himself, in depicting Hamlet, and some authors[1] have

[1] For instance, French: Shakespeareana Genealogica, 1869,
p. 301.

provided us with complete schemes indicating exactly which contemporary figures they surmise to be mirrored in each one in the play. The repeated allusion to the danger of Ophelia's conceiving illegitimately may be connected with both Herbert, who at the time was in prison for being the father of an illegitimate child, and Shakespeare's patron Southampton, who had been permanently dismissed from the Queen's favour in 1598 for hurriedly marrying another Court Lady (Mistress Vernon) to spare her that stigma, as well as the poet himself, who had hastily been married, against his will, in similar circumstances—an act for which he never forgave his wife, and to which we may ascribe some part of his misogyny.

The play that Shakespeare wrote next after "Hamlet" was probably "Measure for Measure", the main theme of which Masson[1] considers to be "mutual forgiveness and mercy". "Julius Caesar", which was probably composed the year before "Hamlet", calls for some special consideration. Here we have a drama apparently devoid of any sexual problem or motive, and yet it has been shown, in Otto Rank's excellent analysis,[2] that the inspiration of the main theme is derived from the same complex as the one we have studied in Hamlet. His thesis is that Caesar represents the father, and Brutus the son, of the typical Oedipus situation. Psycho-analytic work has shown that a ruler, whether king, emperor, president, or what not, is in the unconscious mind a typical father symbol, and in actual life he tends to draw on to himself the ambivalent attitude characteristic of the son's feelings for the father. On the one hand, a ruler may be piously revered, respected, and loved as the wise and tender parent; on the other, he may be hated

[1] Masson: op. cit., p. 133.   [2] Rank: op. cit., S. 204–9.

as the tyrannical authority against whom all rebellion is justified. Very little experience of life is enough to show that the popular feelings about any ruler are always disproportionate, whether they are positive or negative. The most complete nonentity may, if only he finds himself in the special position of kingship, be regarded either as a model of all the virtues, to whom all deference is due, or as a heartless tyrant whom it would be a good act to hurl from his throne. We have pointed out earlier the psychological origin of revolutionary tendencies in the primordial rebellion against the father, and it is with these that we are here mainly concerned. In Hamlet the two contrasting elements of the normal ambivalent attitude towards the father were expressed towards two sets of people; the pious respect and love towards the memory of his father, and the hatred, contempt, and rebellion towards the father-substitutes, Claudius and Polonius. In other words, the original father has been transformed into two fathers, one good, the other bad, corresponding with the division in the son's feelings. With Caesar, on the other hand, the situation is simpler. He is still the original father, both loved and hated at once, even by his murderer. That the tyrant aspect of Caesar, the Caesar who has to be killed by a revolutionary, was in Shakespeare's mind associated with Polonius, another "bad" father who has to be killed, is indicated by a curious identification of the two in the "Hamlet" play: Polonius when asked what part he had ever played answers (Act III, Sc. 2) "I did enact Julius Caesar: I was killed i' the Capitol; Brutus killed me". Those who always underestimate the absolute strictness with which the whole of our mental life is determined will pass this by; to those, however, who are accustomed to trace out the determining factors in unsparing detail it serves as one more example of how fine are the threads connecting our thoughts. Polonius might have quoted any other part on the stage, but it is an unescapable fact that he chose just this one.

Appropriate estimates disclose the curious fact, first pointed out by Craik,[1] that Shakespeare made more frequent allusions to Caesar in his works than to any other man of all past time; of all men in the range of history Caesar seems to have been the one who most fascinated his imagination. There are so many passages mocking at Caesar's hook nose and tendency to brag that Masson[2] concludes these must have constituted special features in Shakespeare's recollection of him. These exhibitionistic symbols accord well with the fact that the boy's "repressed" antipathy towards his father always centres about that part of his father whose functioning most excites his envy and jealousy.

That the two noble characters of Hamlet and Brutus have a great deal in common has often been remarked.[3] The resemblances and differences in which the "son's" attitudes towards the "father" come to expression in the two plays are of very great interest. In "Julius Caesar" they are expressed by being incorporated in three different "sons". Thus, as Rank points out,[4] Brutus represents the son's rebelliousness, Cassius his remorsefulness, and Antony his natural piety,[5] the "father" remaining the same person. In "Hamlet", on the other

[1] Craik: The English of Shakespeare, 3rd Ed., 1864.
[2] Masson: op. cit., p. 177.
[3] See, for instance, by Brandes: William Shakespeare, 1896, p. 456.   [4] Rank: op. cit., S. 209.
[5] Against our treating Brutus, Cassius, and Antony as types in this way it may be objected that they were after all actual historical personages. But we are discussing them as they appear in Shakespeare, to whom they owe most of their life; what we know of them historically is colourless and lifeless by comparison.

hand, the various aspects of the son's attitude are expressed[1] by the device of describing them in regard to three different "fathers", the love and piety towards his actual father, the hatred and contempt towards the father-type Polonius, and the conflict of both towards his uncle-father, Claudius (conscious detestation and unconscious sympathy and identification, one paralysing the other).[2] The parricidal wish in Shakespeare is allowed to come to expression in the two plays by being concealed in two different ways. In "Hamlet" it is displaced from the actual father to the father-substitutes. In "Julius Caesar" there is supposed to be no actual blood relation between the two men, the "son" and "father" types. But a highly significant confirmation of the interpretation here adopted is the circumstance that Shakespeare in composing his tragedy entirely suppressed the fact that Brutus was the actual, though illegitimate, son of Caesar;[3] this fact is plainly mentioned in Plutarch, the source of Shakespeare's plot, one which he almost literally followed otherwise.[4] Even Caesar's famous death-cry "Et tu, mi fili, Brute!" appears in Shakespeare only in the weakened form "Et tu, Brute!". Rank comments on the further difference between the two plays that the son's relation to the mother, the other side of the whole Oedipus complex, is omitted in "Julius

[1] That is, in the main. As is indicated elsewhere in the text, certain "son" aspects are also depicted by, for instance, Laertes.

[2] Hamlet's contrast of the two pictures in the bedroom scene is a perfect delineation of the "good father" and "bad father" as melodramatically imagined by the infant.

[3] Shakespeare's suppressed knowledge, however, seems to leak through in Brutus' apology to Antony for the murder of Caesar (Act III, Sc. 1): "Our reasons are so full of good regard that were you, Antony, the son of Cæsar [i.e. as I am], you should be satisfied".

[4] Delius: "Cäsar und seine Quellen", *Shakespeare-Jahrbuch*, Bd. XVII.

Caesar", whereas, as we have seen, it is strongly marked in "Hamlet". Yet even of this there is a faint indication in the former play. In his great speech to the citizens Brutus says "Not that I loved Caesar less, but that I loved Rome more" (Act III, Sc. 2). Now it is not perhaps altogether without interest in this connection that cities, just like countries, are unconscious symbols of the mother[1]—this being an important source of the conscious feeling of patriotism—so that the passage reads as if Brutus, in a moment of intense emotion, had revealed to his audience the unconscious motive from which his action sprang: to kill the Father who is thought to be ill-treating and tyrannizing over the Mother.

It is appropriate that in both plays the ghost of the murdered ruler appears, in one to the actual murderer (Brutus), and in the other to the avenger, i.e. would-be murderer (Hamlet). In both cases their actions lead to self-destruction. Although dramatically the ghost is another being, psychologically it represents the remorse-ful conscience of the murderer; in Hamlet's case they both bear the same name (an alteration in the original story introduced by Shakespeare).

Besides Shakespeare's obvious interest in Caesar, noted above, there is another set of considerations, some of which were presumably known to Shakespeare, con-necting Brutus and Hamlet, and it seems likely that they constituted an additional influence in determining him to write the one play so soon after the other. They are these. Belleforest[2] pointed out some striking resemblances between Saxo's story of Amleth and the Roman legend of the younger Brutus (Lucius Junius Brutus), and it is

[1] See, for instance, Rank: "Um Städte werben", *Internationale Zeitschrift für Psychoanalyse*, Bd. II, S. 50.
[2] I quote from York Powell in Elton's translation of Saxo's *Danish History*, 1894, pp. 405 et seq.

probable that Saxo derived much of his story from the Latin sources.[1]   Both Plutarch and Belleforest were certainly accessible to Shakespeare. In both cases a son has to avenge a father who had been slain by a wicked uncle who usurped the throne—for the usurper Tarquinius Superbus had slain his brother-in-law, Brutus' father, as well as Brutus' brother[2]—and in both cases the young man feigned madness in order to avoid arousing the suspicions of the tyrant, whom in both cases he finally overthrew. Of further incidental interest, though of course not known to Shakespeare, is the fact that the name Hamlet[3] has the same signification as that of Brutus, both words meaning "doltish", "stupid"; the interest of this fact will be pointed out presently.

There are numerous other indications of the influence of his Oedipus complex throughout Shakespeare's works, especially in the earlier ones—there are actually son-father murders in Henry VI and Titus Andronicus—but since this subject has been dealt with so exhaustively by Rank in his work "Das Inzest-Motiv in Dichtung und Sage" it is not necessary to repeat his discussion of it here.

[1] Saxo's two main sources were the Roman ones (Livy and Valerius Maximus' "Memorabilia") and the Icelandic Hrólf Saga.
[2] Dionysius Halic: Antiquitates Romanae, 1885, Vol. IV, pp. 67, 77.
[3] See Detter: *Zeitschrift für deutsches Altertum*, 1892, Bd. VI, S. 1 et seq.

CHAPTER VII

HAMLET'S PLACE IN MYTHOLOGY

It is for two reasons desirable at this point to interpolate a short account of the mythological relations of the original Hamlet legend, first, so as to observe the personal contribution to it made by Shakespeare, and secondly, because knowledge of it serves to confirm and amplify the psychological interpretation given above.

Up to the present point in this essay an attempt has been made on the whole to drive the argument along a dry, logical path and to show that prior to that given by Freud all the explanations of the mystery end in blind alleys. So far as I can see, there is no escape from the conclusion that the cause of Hamlet's hesitancy lies in some unconscious source of repugnance to his task; the next step of the argument, however, in which a motive for this repugnance is supplied, is avowedly based on considerations not generally appreciated, though I have tried to minimize the difficulty by assimilating the argument to some commonly accepted facts. Now, there is another point of view from which this labour would have been superfluous, in that Freud's explanation would appear directly obvious. To anyone familiar with the modern interpretation, based on psychoanalytic researches, of myths and legends, that explanation of the Hamlet problem would immediately occur on the first reading through of the play. The reason why this strong statement can be made is that the story of

Hamlet is merely an unusually elaborated form of a vast group of legends, the psychological significance of which is now, thanks to Freud and his co-workers, well understood.

A word is in place here concerning the psychological significance of myths. Much scholarly work has succeeded in classifying them, and also fairy-tales, into a number of groups, each group containing many variants. If now the contents of these groups are analysed they are found to relate to a relatively small number of primordial themes: furthermore, themes that are pretty evidently derived from corresponding infantile phantasies[1]—though, of course, decked out as all conscious products of unconscious phantasy are and also mingled with allusions to events and persons in the external world. It is often possible to know the route whereby a typical story has wandered from one part of the world to another, but that does not seem so important as the matter of its being accepted by the imagination of its new recipients. There appear, therefore, to be a few fundamental themes common to the instinctual life of the race—a state of affairs for which Jung has coined the somewhat ambiguous phrase "collective unconscious" —and one of their modes of expression, by no means entirely out of date, has always been the creation of myths, legends, stories, and so on.

It would exceed our purpose to discuss in detail the historical relationship of the Hamlet legend to the other members of this group,[2] and I shall content myself here with pointing out the psychological resemblances;

[1] See K. Abraham: Traum und Mythus, 1909, and F. Riklin: Wunscherfüllung und Symbolik im Märchen, 1908.

[2] See Zinzow: Die Hamlet-Sage an und mit verwandten Sagen erläutert. Ein Beitrag zum Verständnis nordisch-deutscher Sagendichtung, 1877.

Jiriczek[1] and Lessmann[2] have adduced much evidence
to show that the Norse and Irish variants of it are
descended from the ancient Iranian legend of Kaikhosrav, and there is no doubt of the antiquity of the
whole group, some members of which can be traced
back to the beginning of history. Striking cousins to the
Iranian legend may be found in that of Cirakarin in the
Mahabharata[3] and in fusions of the Greek Bellerophon
saga with the Roman Brutus one.[4] A typical example is
the Finnish legend of Kullero.[5] This hero had the task
of avenging his father, who had been murdered by the
latter's brother. He is exposed as a baby, but grows up,
and on his way to find his uncle and obtain his revenge
he finds a girl in the wood (as does Hamlet in the old
Saxo version). After she has been seduced she discovers
she is the hero's sister (a theme also found in the old
Hamlet saga) and *drowns* herself. The hero feigns madness to deceive his uncle, but fails to achieve his purpose
and commits suicide on the same spot as his sister.

The fundamental theme common to all the members
of the group[6] is the success of a young hero in displacing
a rival father. In its simplest form the hero is persecuted by a tyrannical father, who has usually been

---

[1] Jiriczek: "Hamlet in Iran", *Zeitschrift des Vereins fur Volkskunde*,
1900, Bd. X. S. 353.
[2] Lessmann: Die Kyrossage in Europa. Wissenschaftliche Beilage
zum Jahresbericht der städtischen Realschule zu Charlottenburg,
1906.
[3] Discussed by C. Fries: "Ein indischer Hamlet", *Shakespeare
Jahrbuch*, 1911, Bd. XLVII, S. 195.
[4] R. Zenker: Boeve-Amlethus, Das altfranzösische Epos von
Boeve de Hamtone und der Ursprung der Hamletsage, 1905.
[5] E. N. Setälä: Kullero-Hamlet. Ein sagenvergleichender Versuch,
1911.
[6] In the exposition of this group of myths I am largely indebted
to Otto Rank's excellent volume, Der Mythus von der Geburt des
Helden, 1909, in which most of the original references may also be
found.

warned of his approaching eclipse, but after marvellously escaping from various dangers he avenges himself, often unwittingly, by slaying the father. The persecution mainly takes the form of attempts to destroy the hero's life just after his birth, by orders that he is to be drowned, exposed to cold and starvation, or otherwise done away with. A good example of this simple form, illustrating all the features just mentioned, is the Oedipus legend, from which of course is derived the technical term "Oedipus complex" so familiar in modern psychopathology. The underlying motive is openly betrayed by the hero marrying his mother Jocasta after having slain his father. This incestuous marriage also takes place in the same circumstances in the many Christian versions of the legend, for example, in those pertaining to Judas Iscariot and St Gregory.

The intimate relation of the hero to the mother may be indicated in other ways than marriage, for instance by their both being persecuted and exposed together to the same dangers, as in the legends of Feridun, Perseus, and Telephos. In some types of the story the hostility to the father is the predominating theme, in others the affection for the mother, but as a rule both of these are more or less plainly to be traced.

The elaboration of the more complex variants of the myth is brought about chiefly by three factors, namely: an increasing degree of distortion engendered by greater psychological "repression"; complication of the main theme by subsidiary allied ones; and expansion of the story by repetition due to the creator's decorative fancy. In giving a description of these three processes it is difficult sharply to separate them, but they are all illustrated in the following examples.

The *first*, and most important disturbing factor, that

of more pronounced "repression", manifests itself by the same mechanisms as those described by Freud in connection with normal dreams,[1] psychoneurotic symptoms, etc. The most interesting of these mechanisms of myth formation is that known as "decomposition", which is the opposite of the "condensation" so characteristic of dreams. Whereas in the latter process attributes of several individuals are fused together in the creation of one figure, much as in the production of a composite photograph, in the former process various attributes of a given individual are disunited, and several other individuals are invented, each endowed with one group of the original attributes. In this way one person of complex character is dissolved and replaced by several, each of whom possesses a different aspect of the character which in a simpler form of the myth was combined in one being; usually the different individuals closely resemble one another in other respects, for instance in age. A great part of Greek mythology must have arisen in this way. A good example of the process in the group now under consideration is seen by the figure of a tyrannical father becoming split into two, a father and a tyrant. We then have a story told about a young hero's relation to two older men, one of whom is a tender father, the other a hated tyrant. The resolution of the original figure is often not complete, so that the two resulting figures stand in a close relationship to each other, being indeed as a rule members of the same family. The tyrant who seeks to destroy the hero is then most commonly the grandfather, as in the legends of the heroes Cyrus, Gilgam, Perseus, Telephos, and others, or the grand-uncle, as in those of Romulus and Remus and their Greek predecessors Amphion and Zethod. Less often is he the uncle, as in

[1] Cp. Abraham: Traum und Mythus, 1908.

the Hamlet[1] and Brutus legends, though there is an important Egyptian example in the religious myth of Horus and his uncle Set.[2]

When the decomposition is more complete the tyrant is not of the same family as the father and hero, though he may be socially related, as with Abraham, whose father Therach was the tyrant Nimrod's commander-in-chief. The tyrant may, however, be apparently a complete stranger, as in the examples of Moses and Pharaoh, Feridun and Zohâk, Jesus and Herod,[3] and others. It is clear that this scale of increasing decomposition corresponds with, and is doubtless due to, further stages of "repression"; the more "repressed" is the idea that the father is a hateful tyrant, the more completely is the imaginary figure of the persecuting tyrant dissociated from the recognized father. In the last two instances, and in many others, there is a still higher degree of "repression", for not only are the mother and son, but also the actual father himself, persecuted by the tyrant; it will be recalled how Jesus, Joseph, and Mary all fled together to Egypt from Herod, and when we think that the occasion of the flight was the parents' desire to save their son from the tyrant it is impossible to conceive a more complete dissociation of the loving, solicitous father from the figure of the dreaded tyrant.

There is an even more disguised variant yet, however,

[1] When Amleth kills Feng (Claudius) in the pre-Shakespearean Saxo story he emphasizes the tyrannical nature of his opponent in a speech to the people when he tells them of their relief from the "oppressor's yoke" and adds, "I have stripped you of slavery and clothed you with freedom". (Quoted from I. Gollancz's edition of Saxo in his Sources of Hamlet, 1926.)

[2] Flinders Petrie: The Religion of Ancient Egypt, 1908, p. 38.

[3] Robert Graves, it is true, has recently argued at great length in his King Jesus, 1946, that Jesus was the grandson of Herod—an interesting assimilation to the more standard theme mentioned above.

in which the loving father is not only persecuted by the tyrant, typically in company with the son and mother, but is actually slain by him. In this variant, well represented by the Feridun legend, the son adores his father and avenges his murder by killing their common enemy. It is of special interest to us here because it is the original form of the Hamlet legend as narrated by Saxo Grammaticus, where Feng (Claudius) murders his brother Horwendil and marries the latter's wife Gerutha, being slain in his turn by Amleth. The dutiful Laertes springing to avenge his murdered father Polonius is also an example of the same stage in the development of the myth. The picture here presented of the son as avenger instead of slayer of the father illustrates the highest degree of psychological "repression", in which the true meaning of the story is concealed by the identical mechanism that in real life conceals "repressed" hostility and jealousy in so many families, namely, the exactly opposite attitude of exaggerated solicitude, care, and respect. Nothing is so well calculated to conceal a given feeling as to emphasize the presence of its precise opposite; one can imagine the bewilderment of an actual Feridun, Amleth, or Laertes if they were told that their devotion to their father and burning desire to avenge his murder constituted a reaction to their own buried death-wishes! There could be no more complete repudiation of the primordial hostility of the son.

Yet even in this form of the legend the "repressed" death-wish does after all come to expression; the father is really murdered, although at the hands of a hated tyrant. Myths are like dreams in being only products of the imagination, and if a man who was being psychoanalysed were to dream that a third person murdered his father he would not long be able to blame the third person for the idea, which obviously arose in his *own* mind. The process constitutes psychologically what Freud has termed "the return of the repressed". In spite of the most absolute conscious repudiation of a death-wish the death does actually come about. From this point of view it must be said that the "tyrant" who commits the murder is a substitute for the son who repudiates the idea: Zohâk, who kills Feridun's father Abtin, is a substitute for Feridun, Feng for Amleth, and, in the Polonius section of Shakespeare's drama, Hamlet for Laertes. So that the figure of the "tyrant" in this exceedingly complex variant of the myth is really a compromise-formation representing at one and the same time the hated father and the murderous son. On the one side he is identified with the primordial father, being hated by the young hero who ultimately triumphs over him; on the other with the young hero himself, in that he kills the hero's father.[1]

In Shakespeare's modification of the Hamlet legend there is a still more complicated distortion of the theme, the young hero now shrinking from playing the part of the avenging son. Psychologically it betokens not a further degree of "repression", but rather a "regression". The son really refuses to repudiate the murder-wish; he cannot punish the man who carried it out. Claudius is identified with the son almost as much as with the primary father-figure[2] of the myth. Shakespeare's marvellous intuition has, quite unconsciously, penetrated

[1] For this reason Claudius should always be cast as midway in age between the two Hamlets, linking both together psychologically; in a recent London production, by William Poel, this was done, Claudius appearing about ten years only older than Hamlet.

[2] In the First Quarto Hamlet five times addressed Claudius as father. Shakespeare excised the passages in the Second Quarto and the Folio; they were too near the truth!

beneath the surface of the smooth Amleth version. He lifts for us at least one layer of the concealing "repression" and reveals something of the tumult below.[1]

Not only may the two paternal attributes mentioned above, fatherliness and tyranny, be split off so as to give rise to the creation of separate figures, but others also. For instance, the power and authority of the parent may be incorporated in the person of a king or other distinguished man, who may be contrasted with the actual father.[2] In the present legend, as has already been indicated, it is probable that the figure of Polonius may be thus regarded as resulting from "decomposition" of the paternal archetype, representing a certain group of qualities which the young not infrequently find an irritating feature in their elders. The senile babbler, concealed behind a show of fussy pomposity, who has developed a rare capacity to bore his audience with the repetition of sententious platitudes; the prying busybody whose meddling is, as usual, excused by his "well-meaning" intentions, constitutes a figure that is sympathetic only to those who compassionately recall his bygone capacities and services.[3] Because of his greater distance from the original Oedipus situation, not being a member of the royal family, he draws on to himself the son-hero's undisguised dislike, untempered by any doubts or conflicts, and Hamlet finds it possible to kill him without remorse. That he is but a substitute for

---

[1] One or two friends have reproached me that my work on Hamlet diminished their aesthetic appreciation of the play. I cannot but think, however, that a fuller understanding of Shakespeare's work, its profound truth, its psychological correctness throughout, the depth of its inspiration, must enormously heighten our appreciation of its wonder.

[2] The best example of this is to be found in the Jesus story.

[3] Coleridge declaimed against the custom, evidently prevalent even in his day, of depicting Polonius as a figure of fun.

the step-father, i.e. a father *imago*, is shown by the ease with which the two are identified in Hamlet's mind: after stabbing him he cries out "Is it the king?" although he knows it cannot be.

The *second* disturbing factor in the primary Oedipus scheme is that due to the interweaving of the main theme of jealousy and incest between parent and son with others of a similar kind. We noted above that in the simplest form of decomposition of the paternal attributes the tyrannical rôle is most often relegated to the grand-father. It is no mere chance that this is so, and it is by no means fully to be accounted for by incompleteness of the decomposition. There is a deeper reason why the grand-father is peculiarly suited to play the part of tyrant, and this will be readily perceived when we recollect the large number of legends in which he has previously interposed all manner of obstacles to the marriage of his daughter, the future mother. He opposes the advances of the would-be suitor, sets in his way various conditions and tasks apparently impossible of fulfilment—usually these are miraculously carried out by the lover—and even as a last resort locks up his daughter in an inaccessible spot, as in the legends of Gilgam, Perseus, Romulus, Telephos, and others. The underlying motive in all this is that he grudges giving up his daughter to another man, not wishing to part with her himself (father-daughter com-plex). We are here once more reminded of events that may be observed in daily life by those who open their eyes to the facts, and the selfish motive is often thinly enough disguised under the pretext of an altruistic solicitude for the daughter's welfare; Gretna Green is a repository of such complexes. In two papers giving an analysis of parental complexes[1] I have shown that they

[1] "The Significance of the Grandfather for the Fate of the

are ultimately derived from infantile ones of the Oedipus type, the father's complex in regard to his daughter, called by Putnam[1] the "Griselda complex",[2] being a later development and manifestation of his own original Oedipus complex for his mother.

When his grandfather's commands are disobeyed or circumvented his love for his daughter turns to bitterness and he pursues her and her offspring with insatiable hate. When the grandson in the myth, the young hero, avenges himself and his parents by slaying the tyrannical grandfather it is as though he realized the motive of the persecution, for in truth he slays the man who endeavoured to possess and retain the mother's affections, i.e. his own rival. Thus in this sense we again come back to the primordial father, for whom to him the grandfather is but an *imago*, and see that from the hero's point of view the distinction between father and grandfather is not so radical as it might at first sight appear. We perceive, therefore, that for two reasons this resolution of the original father into two persons, a kind father and a tyrannical grandfather, is not a very extensive one.

The foregoing considerations throw more light on the figure of Polonius in the present play. In his attitude towards the relationship between Hamlet and Ophelia are many of the traits that we have just mentioned as being characteristic of the father-daughter complex displayed by the grandfather of the myth, though by the mechanism of rationalization they are here skilfully

---

Individual" and "The Phantasy of the Reversal of Generations", Ch. XXXVII and XXXVIII of my Papers on Psycho-Analysis, 1938.

[1] J. J. Putnam: "Bemerkungen über einen Krankheitsfall mit Griselda-Phantasien", *Internationale Zeitschrift für Psychoanalyse*, 1913, Bd. I, S. 205; reprinted in his Addresses on Psycho-Analysis, 1921.

[2] See O. Rank: "Der Sinn der Griseldafabel", *Imago*, 1912, Bd. I, S. 34.

disguised under the guise of worldly wise advice. Hamlet's resentment against him is thus doubly conditioned, in that first Polonius, through the mechanism of "decomposition", personates a group of obnoxious elderly attributes, and secondly presents the equally objectionable attitude of the dog-in-the-manger father who grudges to others what he possesses but cannot himself enjoy. In this way, therefore, Polonius represents the antipathetic characteristics of both the father and the grandfather of mythology, so we are not surprised to find that, just as Perseus "accidentally" slew his grandfather Acrisios, who had locked up his daughter Danae so as to preserve her virginity, so does Hamlet "accidentally" slay Polonius, by a deed that resolves the situation as correctly from the dramatic as from the mythological point of view. With truth has this act been called the turning-point of the play, for from then on the tragedy relentlessly proceeds with ever-increasing pace to its culmination in the doom of the hero and his adversary.

The characteristics of the father-daughter complex are also found in a similar one, the brother-sister complex. As analytic work shows every day, this also, like the former one, is a derivative of the fundamental Oedipus complex. When the incest barrier develops early in the life of the young boy it begins first in regard to his relationship with the mother, and only later sets in with the sister as well; indeed, erotic experiences between brother and sister in early childhood are exceedingly common. The sister is usually the first replacement of the mother as an erotic object; through her the boy learns to find his way to other women. His relationship to his sister duplicates that of the two parents to each other, and in life he often plays a father-part in regard to her (care, protection, etc.). In the present play the attitude of Laertes towards his sister Ophelia is quite indistinguishable from that of their father Polonius.

Hamlet's relation to Laertes is, mythologically speaking, a double one, a fusion of two primary Oedipus schemes, one the reverse of the other. On the one hand Laertes, being identified with the old Polonius in his attitude towards Ophelia and Hamlet, represents the tyrant father, Hamlet being the young hero; Hamlet not only keenly resents Laertes' open expression of his devoted affection for Ophelia—in the grave scene—but at the end of the play kills him, as he had killed Polonius, in an accurate consummation of the mythological motive. On the other hand, however, as was remarked earlier, from another point of view we can regard Hamlet and Polonius as two figures resulting from "decomposition" of Laertes' father, just as we did with the elder Hamlet and Claudius in relation to Hamlet. For in the relationship of the three men Hamlet kills the father Polonius, just as the tyrant father kills the good father in the typical Feridun form of the myth, and Laertes, who is from this point of view the young hero, avenges this murder by ultimately slaying Hamlet. An interesting confirmation of this view that the struggle between the two men is a representation of a father-son contest has been pointed out by Rank.[1] It is that the curious episode of the exchange of rapiers in the fatal duel is an evident replacement of a similar episode in the original saga, where it takes place in the final fight between Hamlet and his step-father, when Hamlet kills the latter and escapes unwounded. From this point of view we reach the interesting conclusion that Laertes and Claudius are psychological and mythological equivalents or duplicates.

[1] Rank: Das Inzestmotiv in Dichtung und Sage, 1912, S. 226, 227.

Each represents aspects of both generations, the father who is to be killed and the revolutionary, murderous son, thus differing from Polonius, the Ghost, and the elder Hamlet himself, who are all pure father-figures. The equivalence of the two men is well brought out dramatically. Not only does the King's sword of the saga become Laertes' rapier in the play, but in the duel scene it is evident that Laertes is only a tool in Claudius' hand, carrying out his intention with what was his own weapon. Throughout the play, therefore, we perceive the theme of the son-father conflict recurring again and again in the most complicated interweavings.

That the brother-sister complex was operative in the original Hamlet legend also is evidenced in several ways. From a religious point of view Claudius and the Queen stood to each other in exactly the same relationship as do brother and sister, which is the reason why the term "incestuous" is always applied to it and stress laid on the fact that their guilt exceeded that of simple adultery.[1] Of still more interest is the fact that in the saga—plainly stated in Saxo and indicated in Belleforest—Ophelia (or rather her nameless precursor) was said to be a foster-*sister* of Amleth; in the still earlier Norse source which served Saxo, the Skaane, she is actually the hero's sister,[2] and this was evidently the original pattern of the mythological theme. Mythologically we have therefore to equate the Claudius(=Hamlet)–Gertrude relationship with the Laertes(=Hamlet)–Ophelia one. This incestuous brother-sister theme is evidently a derivative of the son-mother one, as it commonly is in the normal

[1] It may be noted that Shakespeare accepted Belleforest's alteration of the original Saxo saga in making the Queen commit incest during the life of her first husband.

[2] Kemp Malone: "The Literary History of Hamlet", *Anglistische Forschungen*, 1925, Heft 59.

development of the individual. Although it comes to more open expression in some versions of this group, e.g. the legends of Cyrus, Karna, and others, it is unmistakable enough with Hamlet. Ophelia bore in the saga no relation to Polonius, this being an addition made by the dramatist with an obvious motivation. That being so, we would seem to trace a still deeper reason for Hamlet's misogynous turning from her and for his jealous resentment of Laertes' passion over Ophelia.

The *third* factor to be considered is the process technically known to mythologists as "doubling" of the principal characters. The chief motive for its occurrence seems to be the desire to exalt the importance of these, and especially to glorify the hero, by decoratively filling in the stage with lay figures of colourless copies whose neutral movements contrast with the vivid activities of the principals; this duplication or repetition is more familiar in music than in other products of the imagination. This third factor is sometimes hard to distinguish from the first one, for it is plain that a given multiplying of figures may serve at the same time the function of decomposition and that of doubling. In general, it may be said that the former function is more often fulfilled by the creation of a new person who is related to the principal character, the latter by the creation of one who is not; but the rule has many exceptions. In the present legend Claudius seems to subserve both functions.

It is interesting to note that in many legends it is not the father's figure who is doubled by the creation of a brother, but the grandfather's. This is so in some versions of the Perseus legend and, as was referred to above, in those of Romulus and Amphion; in all three of these the creation of the king's brother, as in the Hamlet legend, subserves the functions of both decomposition and doubling. Good examples of the simple doubling process are seen with the maid of Pharaoh's daughter in the Moses legend and in many of the figures of the Cyrus one.[1] Perhaps the purest examples in the present play are the colourless copies of Hamlet presented by the figures of Horatio, Marcellus, and Bernardo; the first of these was derived from a foster-brother of Hamlet's in the saga, doubtless originally an actual brother. Laertes and the younger Fortinbras, on the other hand, are examples of both doubling and decomposition of the main figure. Laertes is the more complex figure of the two, for in addition to representing, as Claudius also does, both the son and father aspects of Hamlet's mentality, in the way explained above, he evinces also the influence of the brother-sister complex and in a more positive form than does Hamlet. Hamlet's jealousy of Laertes' interference in connection with Ophelia is further to be compared with his resentment at the meddling of Guildenstern and Rosencrantz. They are therefore only copies of the Brother of mythology and, like him, are killed by the Hero. Common to Hamlet, Laertes, and Fortinbras is the theme of revenge for murder or injury done to a dead father. It is noteworthy that neither of the latter two show any sign of inhibition in the performance of this task and that with neither is any reference made to his mother. In Hamlet, on the other hand, in whom "repressed" love for the mother is at least as strong as "repressed" hostility against the father, inhibition appears.

The interesting subject of the actual mode of origin of myths and legends, and the relation of them to infantile phantasies, will not here be considered,[2] since our interest

---

[1] This is very clearly pointed out by Rank: Der Mythus von der Geburt des Helden, 1909, S. 84, 85.

[2] Those who wish to pursue the subject from the psycho-analytical

in the topic is secondary to the main one of the play of "Hamlet" as given to us by Shakespeare. Enough perhaps has been said of the comparative mythology of the Hamlet legend to show that in it are to be found ample indications of the working of all forms of incestuous phantasy. We may summarize the foregoing consideration of this aspect of the subject by saying that *the main theme of this story is a highly elaborated and disguised account of a boy's love for his mother and consequent jealousy of and hatred towards his father*; the allied one in which the brother and sister respectively play the same part as the father and mother in the main theme is also told, though with subordinate interest.

Last of all in this connection may be mentioned a matter which on account of its general psychological interest has provoked endless discussion, namely Hamlet's so-called "simulation of madness". I do not propose to review the extraordinarily extensive literature that has grown up over this matter,[1] for before the advent of the new science of psychopathology such discussions were bound to be little better than guesswork and now possess only an historical interest. There is, of course, no question of insanity in the proper sense of the word; Hamlet's behaviour is that of a psychoneurotic, and as such naturally aroused the thought on the part of those surrounding him that he was suffering from some inner affliction. The traits in Hamlet's behaviour that are commonly called "feigning madness" are brought to expression by Shakespeare in such a refined and subtle manner as to be not very transpicuous unless one com-

point of view are referred to the writings of Freud, Rank, and Abraham.

[1] The earlier part of this will be found in Furness' Variorum Shakespeare, "Hamlet", Vol. II, pp. 195–235. See further Delbrück: Über Hamlets Wahnsinn, 1893.

pares them with the corresponding part of the original saga. The fine irony exhibited by Hamlet in the play, which enables him to express contempt and hostility in an indirect and disguised form—beautifully illustrated, for instance, in his conversations with Polonius—is a transmutation of the still more concealed mode of expression adopted in the saga, where the hero's audience commonly fails to apprehend his meaning. He here combines a veiled form of speech, full of obvious equivocations and intent to deceive, with a curiously punctilious insistence on verbal truthfulness. Saxo gives many examples of this and adds:[1] "He was loth to be thought prone to lying about any matter, and wished to be held a stranger to falsehood; and accordingly he mingled craft and candour in such wise that, though his words did not lack truth, yet there was nothing to betoken the truth and betray how far his keenness went". Even in the saga, however, we read[2] that "some people, therefore, declared that his mind was quick enough, and fancied that he only played the simpleton in order to hide his understanding, and veiled some deep purpose under a cunning feint". The King and his friends applied all sorts of tests to him to determine this truth, tests which of course the hero successfully withstands. It is made plain that Amleth deliberately adopts this curious behaviour in order to further his scheme of revenge, to which—thus differing from Hamlet—he had whole-heartedly devoted himself. The actual mode of operation of his simulation here is very instructive to observe, for it gives us the clue to a deeper psychological interpretation of the process. His conduct in this respect has three characteristics: first, the obscure and disguised manner of speech just

[1] Saxo Grammaticus: Danish History, translated by Elton, 1894, p. 109.   [2] Saxo: op. cit., p. 108.

referred to, secondly, a demeanour of indolent inertia and general purposelessness, and thirdly, conduct of childish and at times quite imbecillic foolishness (*Dummstellen*); the third of these is well exemplified by the way in which he rides into the palace seated backwards on a donkey, imitates a cock crowing and flapping its wings, rolling on the floor, and similar asininities. His motive in so acting was, by playing the part of a harmless fool, to deceive the King and court as to his projects of revenge, and unobserved to get to know their plans and intentions; in this he admirably succeeded. Belleforest adds the interesting touch that Amleth, being a Latin scholar, had adopted this device in imitation of the younger Brutus: as was remarked earlier, both names signify "doltish", "stupid"; the derived Norwegian word "amlod" is still a colloquialism for "fool".[1] Belleforest evidently did not know how usual it was for famous young heroes to exhibit this trait; similar stories of "simulated foolishness" are narrated of David, Moses, Cyros, Kaikhosrav, William Tell, Parsifal, and many others besides Hamlet and Brutus.[2]

The behaviour assumed by Amleth in the saga is not that of any form of insanity. It is a form of syndrome well known to occur in hysteria to which various names have been given: "simulated foolishness" (Jones), "Dummstellen", "Moria" (Jastrowitz), "ecmnésie" (Pitres), "retour à l'enfance" (Gandy), "Witzelsucht" (Oppenheim), "puérilisme mental" (Dupré), and so on. I have published elsewhere[3] a clinical study of the

[1] Assen: Norsk Ordbog, 1877.
[2] See Rank: Das Inzest-Motiv, S. 264, 265.
[3] "Simulated Foolishness in Hysteria", *American Journal of Insanity*, 1910; reprinted as Ch. XXV of my Papers on Psycho-Analysis, 3rd Ed., 1923.

condition, with a description of a typical case; Rank[1] has reached similar conclusions from his extensive mythological studies. The complete syndrome comprises the following features: foolish, witless behaviour, an inane, inept kind of funniness and silliness, and childishness. Now, in reading the numerous examples of Amleth's "foolish" behaviour as narrated by Saxo, one cannot help being impressed by the *childish* characteristics manifested throughout in them. His peculiar riddling sayings, obviously aping the innocence of childhood, his predilection for dirt and for smearing himself with filth, his general shiftlessness, and above all the highly characteristic combination of fondness for deception as a thing in itself (apart from the cases where there is a definite motive) with a punctilious regard for verbal truth, are unmistakably childish traits. The whole syndrome is an exaggeration of a certain type of demeanour displayed at one time or another by most children, and psycho-analysis of it has demonstrated beyond any doubt that their motive in behaving so is to simulate innocence and often extreme childishness, even "foolishness", in order to delude their elders into regarding them as being "too young to understand" or even into altogether disregarding their presence. The purpose of the artifice is that by these means children can view and overhear various private things which they are not supposed to. It need hardly be said that the curiosity thus indulged in is in most cases concerned with matters of a directly sexual nature; even marital embraces are in this way investigated by quite young children far oftener than is generally suspected or

[1] Rank: Die Lohengrin-Sage, 1911; "Die Nacktheit in Sage und Dichtung", *Imago*, 1913; numerous passages in his other works previously quoted, especially: Das Inzestmotiv, Der Mythus von der Geburt des Helden, etc.

thought possible. The core of Amleth's attitude is secrecy and spying: secrecy concerning his own thoughts, knowledge, and plans; spying as regards those of his enemy, his stepfather. These two character traits are certainly derived from forbidden curiosity about secret, i.e. sexual matters in early childhood. So is the love of deception for its own sake, a trait which sometimes amounts to what is called pathological lying; it is a defiant reaction to the lies almost always told to the child, and always detected by him. In so behaving the child is really caricaturing the adult's behaviour to himself, as also in the punctiliousness about verbal truth that is sometimes combined with the tendency to deceive; he is pretending to tell the truth as the parent pretended to tell it to him, deceiving going on all the while in both cases. That the theme of the Amleth *motif* is derived from an infantile and sexual source can easily be shown from the material provided in the saga itself. The main test applied to him by Feng in order to discover whether he was really stupid or only pretending to be so was to get a young girl (the prototype of Ophelia) to seduce him away to a lonely part of the woods and then send retainers to spy on them and find out whether he knew how to perform the sexual act or not.[1] Then follows a long story of how Amleth is warned of the plot and manages to outwit the spies and also to attain his sexual goal. This passage, so obviously inappropriate if taken literally as applying to a man of Amleth's age and previous intelligence, can only be understood by correlating it with the unconscious source of the theme, and this always emanates from the impulses of childhood. "Knowledge" is often felt to be synonymous with "sexual knowledge", the two terms being

---

[1] An echo of this is to be found in Polonius' somewhat ambiguous proposal, "I'll loose my daughter to him".

in many contexts interchangeable; for instance, the legal expression "to have knowledge of a girl", the Biblical one "and Adam knew Eve his wife" (after eating of the tree of knowledge), and so on. If a child has mastered the great secret he feels that he knows what matters in life; if he hasn't he is in the dark. And, as in the Amleth saga, to prove that someone is ignorant of this fundamental matter is the supreme test of his stupidity and "innocence".

Spying and overhearing play such a constant part in the Amleth saga as to exclude the possibility of their being unconnected with the central theme of the story. After the plot just mentioned had failed Feng's counsellor, the prototype of Polonius, devises another in which Amleth is to be spied on when talking to his mother in her bedroom. During the voyage to England the King's retainers enter Amleth's bedroom to listen to his conversation. Before this Amleth had spied on his companions and replaced their letter by one of his own. In the later part of the saga, not utilized by Shakespeare, two other instances of spying occur. In "Hamlet" Shakespeare has retained two of these scenes and added one other. The first time is when the interview between Hamlet and Ophelia, doubtless taken from the test described above, is overlooked by the King and Polonius; the second, when Hamlet's interview with his mother is spied on by Polonius, who thereby loses his life; and the third, when the same interview is watched by the Ghost. It is appropriate to the underlying theme of sexual curiosity that two out of these should take place in the mother's bedchamber, the original scene of such curiosity; on both occasions the father or father-substitute comes *between* Hamlet and his mother, as though to separate them, the reversal of a theme common in primitive cosmogonies. The most striking example in "Hamlet" of a spying scene is the famous "play within a play", for in a very neat analysis Rank[1] has shown that this play scene is a disguised representation of the infantile curiosity theme discussed above.

Spying and deception play such a prominent part throughout the play that Gessner[2] is justified in dubbing it "das Schauspiel der Verstellung". As he says: "There is hardly a scene in which deception does not appear on the stage, hardly one of the players who does not hold a mask before his countenance, hardly any respect in which deception fails to appear when it might". One must add that all this deception is not confined to outer aims. As we have seen, with Hamlet it takes above all the form of self-deception, since his anguished struggle is to prevent himself from knowing the horrors in his soul.

From this point of view also we can specify more nearly the precise aspect of the father that is represented by the "decomposed" figure Polonius, who spies on Hamlet in his critical interviews with the two women of his life, Ophelia and his mother. It is clearly the spying, watching, "all-knowing" father, who is appropriately outwitted by the cunning youth. Now it is interesting that, apart from Falstaff and the subordinate names of Reynaldo and Gonzago,[3] Polonius is the only person whose name Shakespeare changed in any of his plays, and one

[1] Rank: "Das 'Schauspiel' in Hamlet", *Imago*, Bd. IV, S. 41.

[2] Th. Gessner: Von welchen Gesichtspunkten ist auszugehen um einen Einblick in das Wesen des Prinzen Hamlet zu gewinnen?", *Shakespeare Jahrbuch*, 1885, Bd. XX, S. 228.

[3] The story of the Gonzago play is taken from a murder by a man of that name of a duke which was committed in 1538 supposedly by means of pouring poison into his ear. I have discussed the significance of this form of murder in a paper "The Death of Hamlet's Father", *International Journal of Psycho-Analysis*, 1949, Vol. XXX.

naturally wonders why he did so. In the Kyd play and
even in the first Quarto the name was Corambis The
suggestion has been made[1] that the name Polonius was
taken from Polonian, the name for a Pole in Elizabethan
English, for the reason that even at that date Poland
was the land pre-eminent in policy and intrigue. The
more generally accepted explanation, however, is that
given by Gollancz,[2] according to which it has reference
to the ideal Counsellor as depicted in a famous work
(De optima senatore, 1568) written by Goslicius, the
greatest Polish statesman of the time.

Amleth's feigned stupidity in the saga is very crudely
depicted and its meaning is quite evident. The use
Shakespeare made of this unpromising material, and the
way in which he made it serve his aim of completely
transforming the old story, is one of the master-strokes
of the drama. Amleth's gross acting, for a quite deliberate
purpose, is converted into a delicately drawn character
trait. Merciless satire, caustic irony, ruthless penetration, together with the old habit of speaking in riddles:
all these betray not simply the caution of a man who has
to keep his secret from those around him, as with
Amleth, but the poignant sufferings of a man who is
being torn and tortured within his own mind, who is
struggling to escape from knowing the horrors of his own
heart. That he was aware of how at moments his suffering had thrown his mind off its balance, so that he
was no longer himself, is shown by his poignant admission
to Laertes in the last Act when for once he speaks pure
truth: one of Dr. Johnson's more stupid comments on

---

[1] By Furness: op. cit., p. 242.
[2] I. Gollancz: "The name Polonius", *Archiv für das Studium der
neueren Sprachen und Literatur*, 1914, Bd. CXXXII, S. 141. See also
A. Brückner: "Zum Namen Polonius", *Archiv*, etc., Bd. CXXXII,
S. 404.

Hamlet condemns him for in this speech lying to the last.

With Amleth the feigned stupidity was the weapon used by a single-hearted man in his fight against external difficulties and deliberate foes; with Hamlet it—or rather what corresponds to it, his peculiar behaviour—was the agent by which the secret of a man torn by suffering was betrayed to a previously unsuspecting foe,[1] and increasing difficulties were created in his path where none before existed. In the issue, Amleth triumphed; Hamlet was destroyed. The different use made of this feature in the story symbolizes more finely than anything else the transformation effected by Shakespeare. An inertia pretended for reasons of expediency becomes an inertia unavoidably forced on the hero from the depths of his nature. In this he shows that the tragedy of man is within himself, that, as the ancient saying goes: Character is Fate. It is the essential difference between prehistoric and civilized man; the difficulties with which the former had to contend came from without, those with which the latter have to contend really come from within. This inner conflict modern psychologists know as neurosis, and it is only by study of neurosis that one can learn the fundamental motives and instincts that move men. Here, as in so many other respects, Shakespeare was the first modern.

[1] On the way in which Hamlet's conduct inevitably led him into ever-increasing danger see Loening, op. cit., S. 385, et seq.

CHAPTER VIII

SHAKESPEARE'S TRANSFORMATION OF HAMLET

IT IS highly instructive finally to review the respects in which the plot of "Hamlet" deviates from that of the original saga. We are here, of course, not concerned with the poetic and literary representation, which not merely revivified an old story, but created an entirely new work of genius. The changes effected were mainly two, and it can be said that Shakespeare was only very slightly indebted to others for them. The first is as follows: In the saga Feng (Claudius) had murdered his brother in public, so that the deed was generally known, and further had with lies and false witnesses sought to justify the deed by pretending it was done to save the Queen from the cruel threats of her husband.[1] This view of the matter he successfully imposed on the nation, so that, as Belleforest has it, "son péché trouva excuse à l'endroit du peuple et fur reputé comme justice envers la noblesse—et qu'au reste, en lieu de le poursuyvre comme parricide[2] et

---

[1] Those acquainted with psycho-analytic work will have no difficulty in discerning the infantile sadistic origin of this pretext (see Freud: Sammlung kleiner Schriften, Zweite Folge, 1909, S. 169). Young children commonly interpret an overheard coitus as an act of violence imposed on the mother, and they are in any case apt to come to this conclusion whichever way they are enlightened on the facts of sex. The belief in question is certainly an aggravating cause of the unconscious hostility against the father.

This point again confirms our conclusion that Claudius partly incorporates Hamlet's "repressed" wishes, for we see in the saga that he not only kills the father-king but also gives as an excuse for it just the reason that the typical son feels.

[2] Saxo also has "parricidium", which was of course occasionally used to denote the murder of other near relatives than the parents.

incestueux, chacun des courtisans luy applaudissoit et le flattoit en sa fortune prospere". Now was the change from this to a secret murder effected by Shakespeare or by Kyd? It is of course to be correlated with the introduction of the Ghost, of whom there is no trace in either Saxo or Belleforest. This must have been done early in the history of the Elizabethan "Hamlet", for it is referred to by Lodge[1] in 1596 and is also found in "Der bestrafte Brudermord", though neither of these reasons is decisive for excluding Shakespeare's hand. But purely literary considerations make it likely enough, as Robertson[2] has pointed out, that the change was introduced by Kyd, who seems to have had a partiality for Ghost scenes. In the saga there was delayed action due to the external difficulties of penetrating through the King's watchful guard. Kyd seems to have retained these external difficulties as an explanation for the delay, though his introduction of the Ghost episode for reasons of his own—probably first in the form of a prologue—somewhat weakened them as a justification, since to have the Ghost episode the murder had to be a secret one—otherwise there would be nothing for the Ghost to reveal and no reason for his appearance. But his Hamlet, as in the saga, had a quite single-hearted attitude towards the matter of revenge; he at once confided in Horatio, secured his help, and devoted himself entirely to his aim. There was no self-reproaching, no doubt, and no psychological problem. Shakespeare, however, saw the obvious advantages of the change in the plot—if he did not introduce it himself—for his intention of transforming the play from an external struggle into an internal tragedy. The change minimizes the external difficulties of Hamlet's

[1] Lodge: loc. cit.
[2] Robertson: op. cit., pp. 44, 55, 56.

task, for plainly it is harder to rouse a nation to condemn a crime and assist the avenger when it has been openly explained and universally forgiven than when it has been guiltily concealed. If the original plot had been retained there would be more excuse for the Klein-Werder hypothesis, though it is to be observed that even in the saga Hamlet successfully executed his task, herculean as it was. The present rendering makes still more conspicuous Hamlet's recalcitrancy, for it disposes of the only justifiable plea for delay. That Shakespeare saw the value of the change thus unwittingly and ununderstandingly introduced by Kyd is proved by the fact that later on he took steps to remove the last traces of even a relative publicity concerning the murder. In the first Quarto Hamlet secures his mother's promise to help him in his plans of revenge, and later Horatio in an interview with the Queen speaks with knowledge of Hamlet's plans of revenge and learns from the Queen that she sympathizes with them. Both these passages were omitted in the second Quarto. The omission unmistakably indicates Shakespeare's intention to depict Hamlet not as a man dismayed by external difficulties and naturally securing the co-operation of those he could trust, but as a man who could not bring himself to speak even to his best friend about his quite legitimate desire for revenge, simply because his own mind was in dire conflict on the matter.

The second and all-important respect in which Shakespeare, and he alone, changed the story and thus revolutionized the tragedy is the vacillation and hesitancy he introduced into Hamlet's attitude towards his task, with the consequent paralysis of his action. In all the previous versions Hamlet was throughout a man of rapid decision and action wherever possible, not—as with

Shakespeare's version—in everything except in the one task of vengeance. He had, as Shakespeare's Hamlet felt he should have, swept to his revenge unimpeded by any doubts or scruples and had never flinched from the straightforward path of duty. With him duty and natural inclination went hand in hand; from his heart he wanted to do that which he believed he ought to do, and thus was harmoniously impelled by both the summons of his conscience and the cry of his blood. There was none of the deep-reaching conflict that was so disastrous to Shakespeare's Hamlet. It is as if Shakespeare, on reading the story, had realized that had *he* been placed in a similar situation he would not have found the path of action so obvious as was supposed, but would on the contrary have been torn in a conflict which was all the more intense for the fact that he could not explain its nature. Bradley, in the passage quoted earlier, might well say that this was the only tragic situation to which Shakespeare himself would not have been equal, and we now know the reason must have been that his penetration had unconsciously revealed to his feeling, though not to his conscious intelligence, the fundamental meaning of the story. His own Oedipus complex was too strong for him to be able to repudiate it as readily as Amleth and Laertes had done, and he could only create a hero who was unable to escape from its toils. Shakespeare had failed in early life to find any solution to the problem of the "eternal triangle" with which every child is faced. For years he had been familiar with the legendary story of Hamlet, the meaning of which his unconscious was gradually divining. Then when the double betrayal by his friend and his mistress broke over him like a thunder-cloud he was unable to deal with it by any action, but it aroused the slumbering associations in his mind, and he responded by creating Hamlet, who expressed for him what he could not express for himself—his sense of horror and failure.

In this transformation Shakespeare exactly reversed the plot of the tragedy. Whereas in the saga this consisted in the overcoming of external difficulties and dangers by a single-hearted hero, in the play these are removed and the plot lies in the fateful unrolling of the consequences that result from an internal conflict in the hero's soul. From the struggles of the hero issue dangers which at first did not exist, but which, as the effect of his untoward essays, loom increasingly portentous until at the end they close and involve him in final destruction. More than this, every action he so reluctantly engages in for the fulfilment of his obvious task seems half-wittingly to be disposed in such a way as to provoke destiny, in that, by arousing the suspicion and hostility of his enemy, it defeats its own purpose and helps to encompass his own ruin. The conflict in his soul is to him insoluble, and the only steps he can make are those which inexorably draw him nearer and nearer to his doom. In him, as in every victim of a powerful unconscious conflict, the Will to Death is fundamentally stronger than the Will of Life, and his struggle is at heart one long despairing fight against suicide, the least intolerable solution of the problem. He is caught by fate in a dilemma so tragically poignant that death becomes preferable to life. Being unable to free himself from the ascendancy of his past he is necessarily impelled by Fate along the only path he can travel—to Death. In thus vividly exhibiting the desperate but unavailing struggle of a strong man against Fate Shakespeare achieved the very essence of the Greek conception of tragedy, but he went beyond this and showed that the essence of man's Fate is inherent in his own soul.

There is thus reason to believe that the new life which Shakespeare poured into the old story was the outcome of inspirations that took their origin in the deepest and darkest regions of his mind. He responded to the peculiar appeal of the story by projecting into it his profoundest thoughts and emotions in a way that has ever since wrung wonder from all who have heard or read the tragedy. It is only fitting that the greatest work of the world-poet should have had to do with the deepest problem and the intensest conflict that have occupied the mind of man since the beginning of time—the revolt of youth and of the impulse to love against the restraint imposed by the jealous eld.

A NOTE ON THE ACTING OF HAMLET

I APPEND here a few merely cursory observations that may be of some interest.

Hamlet plays himself, and an actor must be poor indeed to be a total failure in the part. On the other hand, the figure is so prodigally rich, is charged with such a superabundance of attributes, that it would be unreasonable to expect any one actor to display them all in their full measure. One asks of every actor simply: "What particular aspects did he emphasize?" It is not likely that the gentle melancholiac will make a reappearance; his day is over. The central feature is surely Hamlet's intense suffering, of a special order that cannot be bravely endured. He impulsively seizes at every opportunity to distract his tortured mind, or relieve his emotional tension, since he finds it impossible to find a way forward on which he might concentrate. He is caught in coils from which there is no escape, so with all his penetration and his intensity there can be no sense of consistent power; struggle as he may he is a doomed man.

Among the Hamlets I have seen there stand out in my memory Henry Irving, with his alternation of sudden passionate excitement and restrained intensity; Sarah Bernhardt, with her haunting sense of suffering; Beerbohm Tree, who gave a sentimental presentation; Forbes-Robertson, with his beauty and culture but too sane and reasonable demeanour; H. B. Irving, depicting a weak and resentful Hamlet; Martin Harvey, the romantic; Matheson Lang, the hearty Hamlet; John Gielgud, with his bitter disillusionment, and Laurence Olivier, with his robust vehemence.

Claudius is such a straightforward part that it is usually played to perfection. Gertrude is generally too much the dignified queen. She may be shallow, but sensuality is her outstanding characteristic and that is seldom brought out. Ophelia, too, should be unmistakably sensual, as she seldom is on the stage. She may be "innocent" and docile, but she is very aware of her body. Hamlet himself, on the other hand, may at times be bawdy in a forced fashion but is never sensual—especially towards his mother. Polonius is commonly turned into a buffoon, and his children, who certainly respect and obey him, are mistakenly made to snigger at him during his advice speech. It is only Hamlet who takes an unfavourable view of him, and that for reasons of his own which are far from objective.

Ages.—Every actor must give Hamlet the age that suits him personally, but he should try to keep it within the twenties—preferably the late twenties. I have seen Hamlet played as a callow youth of eighteen and a mature philosopher of forty, both which exceed the permissible limit.

The Ghost should not be above a hundred, as he often is. His suitable age is fifty. Claudius is best at forty and Gertrude at forty-five; she is commonly cast too young, even younger than Hamlet.

Above all I would suggest to producers and actors that it is hopeless merely to read the play as if it were a modern one and to rely on the lines carrying one through. It is a play that needs thought and knowledge to produce intelligently. Since one cannot premise a knowledge of the Elizabethan background, with the wealth of allusions, ambiguities, and archaisms, the sensible thing is to consult someone who has laboriously acquired the knowledge. Fortunately, we now possess just the presentation needed for that purpose in Professor Dover Wilson's "What Happens in Hamlet", and to produce the play without having studied at least this one book is a hardly forgivable presumption.

INDEX

NORTON CRITICAL EDITIONS